ROUND MANHATTAN'S RIM

A FAMILIAR WATERFRONT SCENE
ON THE LOWER END OF THE ISLAND

ROUND
MANHATTAN'S RIM

HELEN WORDEN

Edited by Barbara La Rocco

Going Coastal, Inc.

Library of Congress Control Number: 2024941692

ISBN 978-0-9729-8036-4 (paperback)

First Edition, 1934 by the Bobbs-Merrill Company

Coastal Classics Edition
A project of Going Coastal, Inc.

GOING COASTAL republished Helen Worden's book *Round Manhattan's Rim* to preserve and celebrate the historical and cultural significance of Manhattan's waterfront. This classic work provides a vivid snapshot of New York City's maritime heritage, capturing the vibrancy of its waterfront communities and industries during the early 20th century.

Helen Worden Erskine Cranmer (1896-1984), was a journalist, advice columnist, biographer, and ghostwriter. She worked as a reporter and columnist for *The World* (later *New York World-Telegram*) from 1926 to 1944, contributed freelance work to magazines from 1944 until 1956, worked as associate editor for Collier's from 1952 until 1956, and wrote the Dorothy Dix syndicated advice column from 1959 until 1964. She also published books on New York City and recluses, and served as a ghostwriter for several autobiographies and many biographical and autobiographical magazine articles.

In this literary work, Worden embarked on a captivating journey around the periphery of Manhattan with her friend Mrs. Theodore Steinway, illuminating the diverse communities and cultural landscapes that define the city. Her writing not only provides readers with a vivid portrayal of New York's 1932 waterfront but also captures the romance of the people and the tang of the places that rim the edge of Manhattan Island, along the East, Harlem and Hudson Rivers. She has explored quaint spots, revived past glories, traced amazing changes, and put all into this charming, gossipy guide.

By bringing this book back into circulation, Going Coastal aims to connect modern readers with the rich history of Manhattan's shoreline, fostering a greater appreciation for the evolution of its waterfront and the enduring importance of these coastal areas in shaping the city's identity and growth. This republication also aligns with the organization's mission to promote stewardship and awareness of coastal resources, making this historical narrative accessible to a contemporary audience eager to explore the past and its influence on present-day New York; a companion to the urban waterfront guide, *Going Coastal New York City*.

Going Coastal, Inc. was formed in 2004 to help create positive, enduring change in the world. New experience, travel and discovery changes lives. Through various initiatives, programs, publishing, and partnerships, Going Coastal promotes sustainable travel practices, advocates for responsible coastal development, and fosters a sense of community and stewardship among individuals who share a love for coastal regions. Ultimately, the purpose of Going Coastal, Inc. is to inspire and empower people to connect with, appreciate, and actively contribute to the sustainable future of our coastal areas.

Explore goingcoastal.org to learn more about Manhattan's rim. Discover the fascinating evolution of Manhattan's waterfront by comparing a map of the waterfront circa 1933 with its modern-day counterpart on goingcoastal.org. Uncover the dynamic changes and developments that have shaped this iconic stretch over the decades.

Follow us on social media #exploregoingcoastal

Contents

One

New York's Frontier

THE BATTERY, SOUTH END
OF MANHATTAN
ISLAND.

ROMANCE and adventure lie on the waterfront of a great city.

In the middle, up-to-date buildings obliterate early landmarks. On shoreline streets, you will find the past, as well as the present, see the ever-changing character of the town, and meet the pioneer types of a frontier civilization.

The waterfront of island and river cities is the original part of it. This is particularly true of New York.

The Battery is the gateway to the huge metropolis. Since the landing of the Dutch in 1609, this southernmost section of Manhattan Island has figured constantly in the history of the city of six million.

The Battery is familiar to those who have watched it from ferry boats and ocean liners, contacted it by occasional visits to the Aquarium, and strolled along its wall on summer days.

But it is one of the few New York waterfront localities that is known. How many have seen East Marginal Street with its windswept spaces? Who can tell where Jeffery's Light is, and where would you go to fish for striped bass in Manhattan waters, or set crab traps off the rim of the most important city in the world? Places not hard to find if you look.

So Mrs. Theodore Steinway and I discovered when we set out one May morning to encircle Manhattan Island on foot.

New York is a hobby we share in common. Ruth Steinway comes from an old Knickerbocker family, the Mortons, who made their home on State Street when the Battery was the fashionable part of town. Morton Street is named after them. Born on Murray Hill, Mrs. Steinway has lived on Manhattan Island the greater part of her life. She knows and loves it as few people do.

I have the same affection for New York and, like her, have wandered in and out of its streets.

Deep as our knowledge of the city was, however, we both discovered, on comparing notes, that we knew little of the waterfront.

"Have you ever followed the old Harlem shipping canal?"

Ruth Steinway asked one day, adding vaguely: "I believe there are several interesting spots along the way."

"I've always wanted to know that end of Manhattan Island," I said, "but I've never done anything about it."

Mrs. Steinway called me up the next morning. "Were you really serious? Do you want to see New York from the waterfront?"

"Do you mean follow the shoreline clear round Manhattan Island?"

"Why, yes, I hadn't thought of it that way. But suppose we try it?"

"There's nothing I'd like better," I cried. "When can you start?"

"Tomorrow, if you want to," she said.

Our first walk was on the twenty-second of May, 1933. We finished on the thirteenth of December in the same year. Our wanderings were interrupted by a summer in the country, which was all very well. Hot weather is not conducive to easy walking, as we discovered when Ruth Steinway came in from the country one scorching July day.

May and June are ideal months for walking, and so is October. November and December are cold, and winds are bad, particularly on the riverfront. We did not like the cold days because few people were out of doors. We missed the street life, which is all in the New York picture.

We took ten different days to make the thirty-three miles around the island, sometimes using up a morning, often an entire day.

We made a point, on all of our jaunts, in being a part of the scenery. We never approached any section of town in the spirit of sightseers. The clothes we wore were those we might have slipped on to do neighborhood shopping.

Our cameras, when we did carry them, were so small that they could easily be slipped in pockets. I seldom made notes along the way. People close up like clams at the sight of a pad and pencil.

We stopped wherever we happened to be for a bite of luncheon. Likely as not, it was some hot dog stand or diner. Hamburger sandwiches and a mug of ale were our favorite fare. The most expensive luncheon cost a little over a dollar for the two of us. It was after three in the afternoon and we were very hungry.

We never tucked more than a couple of dollars in our bags. Sometimes we picked up old prints and ship's lanterns in second-hand stores, and so spent our extra change. But if you are interested in seeing the waterfront and feel in a money-saving mood, you can foot it around the island in as modest a way as you wish. Lunches are the only expense.

The day of our first walk was bright and clear, with a fresh wind blowing in from the sea. We met at the Battery around half-past ten and began at once with South Street, which lies on the East Side of Manhattan Island and extends from the Battery to Corlear's Hook Park.

South Street, on the shoreside, is lined with houses that were in existence during clipper-ship times. Sailors from every port in the world bask on its pavements in sunny weather, and quaint little shops peculiar to nautical neighborhoods nestle along its sidewalks.

It is full of color. The Spanish and Portuguese see to that. Bright blue paint is slicked over window sills and doorways.

Vivid scarlet geraniums fill rickety balconies and warm-toned blouses and jeans cover the sailors. Against the weather-beaten red-brick walls of the old houses, this helter-skelter mass of color is primitive in its lushness.

The port of call for sailors is the Seamen's Institute at 25 South Street, a few blocks up from the Battery on the East River. Dr. Archibald Mansfield is the superintendent.

Visitors are welcome. It is a fascinating spot, chockful of stories. The lost and found department will interest you. After three years, I believe, unclaimed articles are turned over to the Institute's museum. Strange things find their way into it: elephant's tusks, opium pipes, brass knuckles, old seamen's chests, sometimes filled with rum and curious Oriental weapons.

Many of the neighborhood people who carry on their lives in the vicinity of the Institute remember when it was a floating church off the foot of Pike Street. It is now a building thirteen stories high with accommodations for two thousand sailors.

The Institute was the outgrowth of a group known as the Young Men's Missionary Society, organized in 1843. It has conducted services in three floating chapels.

In 1858, the Institute opened its first mission rooms on Coenties Slip for the canal boat and harbor-craft seamen. The old slip at this time was a forest of masts. Bowsprits of clipper ships anchored at the docks, projected out over cobblestoned South Street, and the canal boats that brought wheat from the South and West snuggled close to them.

In 1913, through donations made by friends, it was possible to build the thirteen-story structure at 25 South Street. The new home for seamen had accommodations for five hundred with hotel conveniences and opportunities for recreation. With its coming, disappeared the boarding houses from which the sailors were often shanghaied.

During the World War, because of inadequate accommodations, the board of managers drew up plans for an Annex on the site of a notorious water-front saloon that adjoined the Institute. The Annex was completed in the spring of 1929. The delay was due to the difficulty of getting the property from the saloon people.

The twenty-four-hour traffic through the Institute averages from eight to ten thousand seamen. Eighty percent, of the sailors are American citizens. The post office does the business of a town with a population of twenty thousand.

The words "Of New York" are part of the corporate title. There are other Seamen's Church Institutes in other seaport cities, but 25 South Street is the parent organization.

It is conducted for active seamen of every age, race, and creed.

An outstanding character of the Institute is Mother Roper. She is a thin, kindly-faced woman more than middle-aged, who is the director of the Missing Men Department.

I happened to be at the Institute when Bellevue telephoned her. "Your son is dying," a nurse said, "he asked us to call you."

"But I have no son," she protested.

"He says that you're his mother," the nurse persisted.

Mrs. Roper put on her hat and went up to the hospital. The nurse led her to the ward where the sick man lay. He was an old-colored sailor!

"I knew you would come," he said.

Mrs. Roper stayed with him till he died.

The Institute also has its share of comedy. Long John Silver, the barge captain, furnishes some of it. It has been his custom to make his wooden leg the repository for his savings.

"You'd better not try that, John," the cashier at the Institute warned him. "Somebody'll steal your leg."

The Skipper scratched his head and decided to leave the money with the cashier before he went out in Coenties Slip Park to sun himself.

Two hours later, the doorkeeper was aroused by a great shouting and hullabaloo. He ran to the street. There was Long John Silver being carried over from the park by two sailors. While he napped, his wooden leg had been stolen!

The savings that he had left with the cashier, were just enough to pay for a new wooden leg. The little park where Long John suns himself, plus his new wooden leg and minus his savings, faces Patrick O'Connor's clam stand.

Two

Fresh Clams for Sale

THE CLAM MAN

THE FIRST stop we made was at the clam stand. It snuggles below Jeanette Park and South Street alongside the Seamen's Institute. The little wooden shack with its spotless counter has been on this ground since 1849. Two owners, Robert Peach who died in 1919, and Patrick O'Connor, the present proprietor, have guided its destiny.

"Teddy Roosevelt used to come down here for clams," sounded off Mr. O'Connor as he passed each of us out a dish of freshly opened cherry stones. "Lots of Wall Street men look me up. I'm a landmark."

The clam man was born within hailing distance of his stand. As a boy, he went swimming off Battery Park, coaxed apples away from the old fruit woman at Washington Market, and rode horse cars up and down South Street.

O'Connor is Irish. His eyes are blue and his hair is red. He lives on Staten Island but spends most of his time at his clam stand. If you like fresh clams, he sells them for fifteen cents a half-dozen. In winter he sometimes steams clams.

New York has three clam stands. They hug the Battery. William Flanagan owns the first booth at the Battery Wall. He used to be head oysterman at Sherry's. I recommend his clam broth. It is ten cents a cup.

The second clam stand is run by Dave Everett outside the Staten Island Ferry. Patrick O'Connor has the third.

Clam stands are closely associated with the history of New York. The original John Jacob Astor conducted one on the site of the old Dutch fort where the Cunard Building now rises. It was a cozy location with flowers and trees and chairs in a garden.

The products that the clam-stand men sell come from the Fulton Fish Market, Al Smith's Alma Mater. Al Smith calls the Market the finest college in the world. He boasts that he is a graduate of the F. F. M.

A colony that thrived during Mr. Smith's fish market days was the ice barge town. Electrical refrigeration has dealt its citizens a death blow.

"But they're not many of them fellows left now," Patrick O'Connor said, "though you'll still find a few of their boats down off Peck's Slip."

The clam man looked out the window of his little house.

"There's the big barge-town." He pointed to a collection of boats tied alongside one another at the foot of Coenties Slip. "Why don't you go over and have a talk with Black Jim Warren? Tell him I sent you."

"One more cup of clam broth, and then we'll go," I said.

"The same for me" said a tall, lanky young fellow, breezing in the door. "I haven't had any sleep for two nights. Clam broth is a bracer."

"And why haven't ye had any sleep?" inquired O'Connor severely.

The boy gulped the broth. "I drive a truck between here and Cincinnati. I'm making time."

"What do you haul?" I asked.

"Anything," he answered. "Just now it's stuff for the Erie Railroad at sixty cents a hundred."

"Everything's trucking now," said the clam man. "It's done away with coastwise shipping and it's killed things for them barges," nodding again in the direction of the old boats.

"Yep, competition's there all right," admitted the boy. "That's why I drive through without sleeping."

"When do you get caught up?" I questioned.

"Soon as I get back to Cincinnati. I'll sleep for two days straight."

"Aren't you afraid of falling asleep on the road?"

"No. If I feel tired, I pull off to the side."

"Anybody with you?"

"No. I go it alone. I own my own truck."

Our conversation was drowned by the rattle of big and little trucks down South Street. "There go some of your friends," the clam man said. "They stream by here day and night." The boy glanced out. A huge green truck lumbered by.

"Gee! There's a Brockway! I'm going to have one of those soon." He had the look of a man picking a fine racehorse.

"What do you drive now?"

"A Ford. It's over on West Street, loading up. Well, I must be getting going. So long."

The romance of transportation! This was a new touch to the waterfront. First, the fast clipper ships, bound for the Southern States, the California Coast, and New England. Then the steam vessels and barges trailing powerful tugs and now the great trucks.

The boy might have been a reincarnation of a pony express rider streaking it across the country or the youthful Master of a swift, white-winged sailing vessel racing into port.

In contrast to his eager, adventurous spirit, was the sleepy philosophy of the barge captains.

One hundred and seventy-five canal boats rocked gently at the pier, facing Jeanette Park. Men, women, and children swarmed the little two-by-four rooms, stuck like sore thumbs at the barge-boat ends.

None-too-white washing flapped in the wind. An occasional window slid open and a head popped out as we climbed from boat to boat, in search of William Warren.

His elder son welcomed us. "Pa's below," he said. Captain Warren was resting easy near the stove, a leg propped up on a chair. "I broke it eight years ago," he said, "my leg, not the chair. Things haven't gone so well since."

The skipper of Warren Brothers Barge lives aboard with his

two sons, for whom the barge is named. The boat hasn't been out of port on a working errand since 1929.

"And may never go again," said the Captain. "Trucking's cut in on us. We're too slow. That and canal-barge monopoly has finished us."

He drew his ragged brown sweater about him. "My grandfather helped dig the Erie Canal. But that doesn't help us now."

The boys glanced uneasily out of the fly-specked window. The younger could not have been over ten or eleven. The elder was about sixteen.

"Do they go to school ?" I asked.

"Yes, P. S. 29. All the kids on the canals do."

"Where were they born?"

"On a barge, same as I was. This is our life."

A dreary life in port.

"God—if we could once get on the canals again, things would be different," fumed the old Captain.

"How much does it cost to have a tug haul you?"

"Twenty dollars a day."

"Any work here?"

"A little boat repairs—calking, dock jobs, and such. But that isn't living."

"Are there many women on the barges?"

"Plenty. Most the fellows are married. I'm a widower.

If you want to meet a lady, call on Mrs. Poquette, two boats over."

We shook hands with the old Captain and his two boys. They lingered on deck to guide us to the Poquettes.

Nine little children were crowded into the upper room on

the Poquette barge. "We call this a storm house," said a pleasant-faced, gray-haired woman. "And I'm Mrs. Poquette's mother."

The youngsters were her grandchildren. Mrs. Poquette and her husband joined us, as we walked in. "We don't like to be written about," the wife said. "It is not always good."

"Oh, I'm sure this is just a general story," her mother said. "People come down from the papers every so often. I guess we're different."

"No, we're not," said the daughter. "We're just like other people."

The Poquette barge was as orderly as the Warren boat had been untidy. The white-boarded floors looked as if Mrs. Poquette must have scrubbed night and day to keep them in condition. And the children were round-cheeked and healthy-eyed.

"They're never sick," their mother said.

Mr. Poquette is a French Canadian. "My people for three generations, have owned barges," he said proudly.

"So have mine," said Mrs. Poquette.

"Yes," broke in her mother, "we've all spent our lives on the barges. We wouldn't know how to live any other way."

"But they're doomed," mourned Mr. Poquette. "This type of barge will never be used again. It's all right for a houseboat. But that's all."

"What did you have on it?"

"Everything."

"Where to?"

"Any place a canal cut through."

"What hurt your business?"

"Trucking."

Three

A Revolutionary Prison

WHETHER it was a prison or not, no one knows. The legend goes that the grim, gray stone building that we passed on the corner of South Street and de Peyster Lane was a military prison during the Revolutionary War.

It certainly is forbidding enough to have been a soldiers' jail. People in the neighborhood said the de Peysters owned it. We asked Miss Augusta de Peyster if this were true.

"No indeed," she said, "I don't even know anything about the place."

"But you do know the neighborhood," I persisted.

"I often visit the Seamen's Institute on South Street, just a few blocks below," she admitted. "Perhaps that is why people associate me with the locality."

Strange tales are spun around the lonely structure. Solid iron shutters bar the windows. The walls are thick. Some say that it is used for a warehouse now, but that during the Revolutionary War, the British turned it into a prison, and that in it died many a patriot.

The South Street portion of Manhattan Island, in which Ruth Steinway and I began our walk, is rich in romantic history.

Not far from de Peyster Lane on the southeast corner of Fulton and Front Streets is the red-brick Colonial house in which Aaron Burr lodged at the time of his controversy with Alexander Hamilton. And it was to these rooms in this old building that he returned after the fatal duel at Weehawken.

Hiram Nott's general store and pharmacy lay directly under Mr. Burr's apartment, which was reached by an outside stairway. The name of the proprietor who followed Mr. Nott, Dr. S. A. Brown, is lettered in gold on the sign above the entrance. On it is the date 1806.

They say that the store is much older and that among its patrons were George Washington, the Livingstons, and the de Peysters.

Tommie Tucker runs the drugstore today. He has been in it for forty-five years. It is the only job he has ever had.

Brown's was a great place for sailors in clipper-ship times, Captain Ernest Lamb, who stops at Sweet's Hotel, told us.

"I used to send chests over to Brown's to be filled before every voyage. They come in mighty handy."

The Captain, who hails from Down East, sailed as a lad of twenty-two on the bark *Richards Parsons* to Australia in '87.

"We carried everything," he said, "including ice. It was coal from New York to Bangor and then ice for the Indies. But I'm steamboatin' now. Those days have gone." He looked out on South Street, over his steel-rimmed spectacles. "I recollect when there were so many tea clippers in the River that their bowsprits cast shadows over the horse-cars."

The old-time sailing masters still drop anchor at Sweet's.

Many of the tars have turned yacht masters. There's Captain Stoneman who skippered the elder Morgan's yacht, *Corsair,* and Captain Lamb, who sailed a big steam yacht for a wealthy Wall Street man.

The love for the water is in their blood. The fathers of these sailing masters skippered ships, and their sons and grandsons follow the sea.

At Sweet's, we met the square-rigger captains during mealtime in the quaint dining room on the second floor. Between whiles, they play cribbage in the living room overhead.

They all know the Negus Nautical store at 69 Pearl Street about as well as they do Brown's and Sweet's Hotel.

Not far from Brown's drugstore is the office of A. J. Drummond at 47 Fulton Street. It is within sight of the waterfront.

Mr. Drummond and his family have always worked near the river. The whistle of the boats, the grumbling of fog-horns, and the flap of sailing canvas have been woven into the picture of their existence.

Aubrey Drummond is a photographer. His father and grandfather before him were cameramen. Theirs is part of old as well as present-day New York's history. Mrs. Steinway wanted her children to see Mr. Drummond's place. Two of them went with us when we visited the Drummond studio.

The great, old-fashioned rooms, winding stairs leading to them, and Victorian furniture suggest a Dickensian interior.

Among the keepsakes in Mr. Drummond's safe is a cylindrical tin box and a roll of yellow parchment. They came into his family because of his Grandmother Lewis's best black silk skirt. The skirt figured largely in the early history of photography. Mrs. Lewis's husband was the fashionable photographer of the 'sixties, and his studio was the rendezvous for social lights of old New York.

Those were daguerreotype days. The pictures had to be made with a fixed focus. William Henry Lewis, being of an inventive turn of mind, felt he might improve upon the method. He hit on an idea that involved not only the use of lumber but the need of a heavy soft material. In vain he searched for a fabric that was strong and yet supple enough to answer his purpose. None of the department stores, not even Ridley's, had what he wanted. The clerks thought a heavy silk might do. This meant waiting for the arrival of the next packet from the Indies, or China.

Impatient at the delay, Mr. Lewis told his wife of the difficulty. "Take my silk skirt," she said. Her husband objected. But she ripped the black taffeta apart before his eyes. Out of it, he made a collapsible bellows which he attached to the wooden machine that he had constructed. When he finished his strange accordion-like box he mounted it on a trestle that resembled a McCormick reaper.

The first picture taken with it was a success. It revolutionized photography. People flocked from far and wide to see Mr. Lewis's experiment. Fame of it spread to Europe. Queen Victoria heard of the invention. "A man who has that amount of genius should be rewarded," she said. With the proper amount of ceremony, she sent him a note of praise neatly expressed on parchment. It was accompanied by a huge waxen seal nicely packed in a tin cylinder.

Mr. Lewis has been dead for many years. His daughter married Alonzo Drummond, linen merchant. Their son, Alonzo, like his Grandfather Lewis, wanted to take pictures. He made use of Mr. Lewis's old studio and cameras. During the Civil War, he was commissioned to take official pictures of the front. The pass assigned to him by Congress reposes in Aubrey Drummond's safe with the cylinder and parchment.

Aubrey Drummond has the same passion for taking pictures that his father and great-grandfather had. However, he is famed not for his pictures of social celebrities, but for his court work involving the taking of fingerprints and murder scenes. It was his camera that switched evidence in the Hall-Mills murder case. And it is his camera that may turn the tide in the Wendel will lawsuit which involves the old Scotchman, John Morris, now imprisoned on Welfare Island, since the court ruled that he had perjured himself in the Wendel trial.

They say that the oldest drug firm in New York is the Schieffelin Drug Company at 16 Cooper Square. It used to be at 195 Pearl Street, not far from the waterfront, opposite the ancient Fly Market at the foot of Maiden Lane.

William J. Schieffelin who lives at 1165 Park Avenue is the great-great-grandson of Jacob Schieffelin who purchased and continued the drug business of Effingham Lawrence in 1781 at 227 Queen Street. The present Mr. Schieffelin is the head of the firm.

Oliffe's, of course, at Number 6 Bowery, is always pointed out as New York's oldest drug store. But I think Brown's is the oldest retail apothecary shop. Oliffe's opened up business in 1805. The fixtures have never been changed. The same gloomy, mahogany counters, wide-planked floors, and high somber ceilings remain untouched.

Others say that Quackinbush's and not Brown's or Oliffe's should carry the scepter of Father Time. Quackinbush's hangs out a shingle at 703 Greenwich Avenue.

It is one hundred and sixteen years old by record, but even older by legend.

"We'll look it up," Mrs. Steinway suggested, "when we get over on West Street."

Later, we found that the bottles used in Quackinbush's have passed the century mark and so have the prescriptions. A favorite one, still popular, is a corn cure.

Bagoe's drug store at 86 Madison Avenue was the standby of Victorian New York. Mrs. Steinway's mother dealt there. Its interior, especially the white woodwork in the rear, resembles the Leadbeater pharmacy in Alexandria, Virginia, which remained in active use till a few years ago. This was the oldest drugstore in the United States.

Brown's and Oliffe's still boast, as few drug stores do today, the glass jars filled with colored water and illuminated by a small light, for window decorations.

It was these same colored lights at Oliffe's that caused an

old sailor who lives at the Seamen's Institute on South Street, to rush in one night, crying, "Hey! Yer starboard and port lights are mixed. The red's on the wrong side. Ye're liable to cause a collision!"

Four

Bridges

NEW YORK began casting forth slender strands to spin future highways from one shoreline to another in 1870. The great mass of steel cable that spun itself into the Brooklyn Bridge first took root at the foot of Roosevelt Street now the congested Spanish quarter of Manhattan Island which we skirted in stopping to look at the tiny cafes of a Castilian flavor along the waterfront in the vicinity of Brooklyn Bridge. The majority of these old-world eating houses were clustered near Roosevelt Street.

As far back as the eighteenth century, Roosevelt Street figures in the city's slum district. Even then, the flotsam and jetsam of other nations had drifted into the narrow, alley-like thoroughfare.

Many of the houses that sheltered these people were torn down to make way for the Brooklyn Bridge. Few remain. Of those demolished, a number had seen better days, among them, the home of George Washington at Number One Cherry Street. If you walk a few blocks back from the waterfront, you will see the tablet near the bridge that marks the spot where it stood.

Cherry Street was also Alexander Hamilton's neighborhood. He lived in a neatly designed Colonial brick residence at 173 Cherry. It is now Madonna House. The nuns are proud of its former glory. As you follow the waterfront, glance as we did up Market Street. It was Sister Mary Elizabeth who said it once belonged to Alexander Hamilton.

"And Washington has visited here often," she reminded us. "He even sat in this very room," nodding about her at the white walls, high ceilings, and Colonial fireplace.

Number 173 Cherry Street lies now in the heart of Spanish New York. A few blocks to the north are the boundary lines of Little Italy and the Ghetto.

The sidewalks swarm with children, push-carts, and street vendors. A graceful black wrought-iron balustrade defines the steep front steps, which Sister Mary Elizabeth fought to keep the city from removing.

"New York did not think enough of Washington's house at One Cherry Street to preserve it," she said, "but I made up my mind that this place should be kept intact. There are few enough examples of early American architecture as it is."

Sister Mary Elizabeth, with the aid of eleven white-coifed,

black-habited, kindly-faced nuns, takes care of the spiritual and physical wants of Alexander Hamilton's old neighborhood.

"We do everything and anything for the people," she explained, "with no questions asked. Six thousand souls pass through our doors each week. We feed two hundred and fifty children every day. We care for the babies of parents who are out of work, and we have a bread line that takes care of six hundred men every night."

For twenty-three years Madonna House has offered a helping hand to the poor of the Lower East Side. The meal for the children is comparatively recent.

"We had to do it," said Sister Mary Elizabeth, "because so many of the school-children came hungry to their classes."

The first day that the dining room was open two hundred and fifty little boys and girls grouped themselves about the small tables arranged tearoom fashion at Madonna House. There were the usual salt, pepper, sugar, knives and forks, china, and bread on the tables.

After the children had been seated the nuns bustled out into the kitchen to get the soup. When they came back every bit of bread had disappeared; not one piece was left in sight!

"Why, children!" exclaimed Sister Mary Elizabeth, "what has become of the bread?" She looked at them questioningly.

The youngsters pointed to their pockets. "Our mothers and our daddies are hungry," one little boy explained timidly. "We'll have enough to eat, anyway. We are going to take the bread home."

After that, the nuns of Madonna House saw to it that the

children had, in addition to the bread on the table, a supply to give their parents.

Among the friends of Madonna House is Maizie-of-the-Venice, the platinum-haired girl who runs the moving-picture house at 209 Park Row.

"It's nothing to have Maizie drive up here at eleven o'clock at night," said Sister Mary Elizabeth, "and give us money to help some poor family out. She is the most generous soul in the world."

This year the nuns need all the money they can get.

"It takes every cent we can lay our hands on," Sister Mary Elizabeth said, "to run our charities. And even then we have far from enough. There is one family of nine children and the mother and father, who live in a basement near here, are desperately in need of help. I am trying now to get some work for the man. We are tiding them over by having the nine children here for meals."

A little money flows in through the hand-me-down shop conducted for the benefit of Madonna House at Queensboro Market. Several socially prominent women have become interested in it.

The Manhattan Bridge, one block above Madonna House, was completed in 1909, and the Williamsburg Bridge in 1903. The archways of both bridges offer a shelter today to the huge army of "flops," as they are called at the police stations, which drift over to the waterfront from the Bowery. The men look like things dug up from under stones: gray, dusty, bloodless creatures that shrink from the openness of the waterfront. The bridge archways give them a sense of protection. They paid no attention to us when we passed, though when I turned to snap a picture, they were watching us.

We saw many of them in the line that forms in front of Madonna House. With the archways to sleep under, food from Madonna House or some other charity that runs a free kitchen, the Bowery bums manage to get along. Few of them ask for more or want it. Their lives are free of responsibilities, family ties, and the worry of possessions. If pushed, they can wangle a nickel out of Maizie—at the Venice Theater. It usually goes for whisky in one of the Christie Street saloons that serve it raw at five cents a glass.

The streets we walked through touched on Hanover Square. From the very first of Dutch New York history, this section figured in the maritime annals of the thrifty colony. The little square which India House, famous in shipping history, dominates, has always been a center of influence in the town's waterfront affairs.

Hanover Square was, originally, nearly at the water's edge, with a slip running out into the river, we learned by studying old maps. In Dutch Colonial days, it was in sight of the home of Governor Kieff and we discovered that in 1648, this official, tired of feting business guests at home, built the city's first hotel, later on used as the Stadt Huys or City Hall.

The appearance of Manhattan in those early days of Hanover Square has been delightfully described by Madam Knight, an enterprising tourist of the period.

"The buildings are brick, generally," she writes, "in some cases of divers colors and laid in cheques, being glazed, they looked very well." She exclaims over the interiors. "They were neat to admiration." She describes the fireplaces as of tile and extending out into the room. The streets were paved to the width of ten feet from the fronts of the houses, leaving the center unpaved as a runway for water. There were no sidewalks.

The first building on the site of India House on Hanover Square was erected in 1660 by Abraham Martens Clock, miller and carpenter. It was a substantial dwelling, with ground for a vegetable garden and a barn. The property had a well on it to which the neighbors came because of its excellent water. In front ran Burger Jorrison's path from his house to the waterfront.

Nicholas Bayard bought the property in 1673. He tore down the old house and built a more pretentious residence in 1686.

Captain Kidd, who knew his New York waterfront, was a frequent visitor at this home. The famous pirate lived at what is now 56 Wall Street, in a dwelling he bought from Governor Dongan when the wall on Wall Street was torn down.

Freebooters and pirates on the high seas were a constant source of anxiety and loss to the merchants who lived in the Hanover Square neighborhood. The pirates were, in effect, the hijackers of their day. They robbed the slave traders. A boat would go out to get negroes—the pirate would follow it into the remote places where negroes were to be had and there capture the money with which it was intended to buy slaves. This practice became so great a pest that the mercantile interests appealed to the English Ministry to assist them in fitting out a cruising vessel to act against the marauders. Colonel Robert Livingston of New York brought the matter before the English Governor and introduced Captain Kidd to command such a vessel. The undertaking was finally started on a private basis, profits being divided by the owners of the vessels with a liberal share to Captain Kidd.

A commission was issued on December 11, 1695, "To the Trusty and Well Beloved Captain William B. Kidd."

The popular impression has been that Captain Kidd turned pirate and amassed great treasure as a result of his operations. The fact that he was tried in England for piracy, convicted, and hanged gave some authority for this impression. However, recent examinations of records are cited to show that such was not the case; that he was an honest, capable sea captain and that his trial and execution were put through to appease the Grand Mogul who threatened to banish the British from India unless reparation was made for French ships legitimately taken by Kidd under the then existing relations between the two countries, but which contained cargoes shipped by Indian merchants. The matter was discussed in the House of Commons, which threatened to proceed against the owners of Kidd's vessel; but, when it developed that these owners were men high in the King's favor, the Commons hesitated to proceed. Captain Kidd was made the scapegoat and lost both life and reputation so that others might go free.

The New York Title and Mortgage Company has in its possession an abstract of India House property, which goes back to the earliest English days of New York—in other words, to the persons who held the property by grant from the King after the British, for the second time, definitely assumed control of New York.

The first owner of record is a man of that family whose name is still a force in New York, Samuel Bayard. An early glimpse we get of it in the records shows that he lived on Hanover Square with his father, Nicholas Bayard. They were of a fighting family. Their record has left an imprint on New York history.

Nicholas Bayard came to New York when a youth and in 1665 was appointed Clerk of the Court of Mayor and Alderman. At that time there was a great feud between Jacob Leisler and Governor Dongan. Mr. Bayard was a member of the Governor's Council and conspicuous in his opposition to Leisler and those who opposed the Governor. He was banished but returned secretly to get some papers. His presence was made known and Hanover Square was full of men with torches to capture him. He made his escape, however, but was afterward captured and imprisoned for a year. Later on, at the overthrow of Leisler, Bayard was reinstated and succeeded in bringing Leisler to the scaffold.

He died in 1711. The property went to his son, Samuel Bayard, from whom the chain of title in India House begins.

Hanover Square, from the early days of its history, was an important place for the shipping business. Even in 1754, it was an urban center. William Walton, the rich man of his day, gave up his house in Hanover Square to move "well out of town," to Queen Street, which is now about Franklin Square.

It is very probable that the building now standing at One Hanover Square is the first structure that was built on this property as a whole. There were small houses there during the Dutch and Colonial period but whatever stood on this spot was, undoubtedly, burned in the great fire of 1833.

While the tax records of New York City do not go back to this date, other records showing transfers of real estate involved, without describing the buildings thereon, indicate that the present home of India House was built by one Richard Carman in a general reconstruction which followed the big fire in 1837.

The Carman family figured frequently in the records of Long Island. They were prominent, influential people in nineteenth-century New York real-estate history.

Their names appeared in the City Directories between 1835 and 1837—the only Richard was Richard A. Carman of 42 Broadway. We ran into that name again in Harlem. It is probable that the family built the Hanover Square structure for stores and rented them, as no Carman then lived in Hanover Square, according to the City Directories.

India House was certainly standing in 1851 exactly as we now see it. The Hanover Bank which occupied the property at that time has a picture showing that it has remained almost unchanged since that date. The Bank acquired the property in 1851 and occupied half of it for banking purposes. The other part was used by the firm of Robert L. Maitland & Company, tobacco importers.

Hanover Square was named in honor of King George of Hanover. We were told that the Hanover Bank, when it was first organized, planned to call itself the Hanover Square Bank, but later changed its name to the Hanover Bank.

After the Hanover Bank moved, the present India House property fell into the possession of Robert L. Maitland. He was a solid, conservative figure in New York's affairs of two generations ago. He subsequently sold the big gray stone mansion to the New York Cotton Exchange in 1870. W. R. Grace & Company, the importers and exporters, bought it in 1885.

India House, as an organization, came into being in 1914,

when a group of businessmen headed by James A. Farrell and the late Willard Straight, decided to found a meeting place in the interests of foreign trade. The building at One Hanover Square was then vacant, W. R. Grace & Company having recently left the site to move into larger quarters elsewhere on the Square.

India House rented the building from George Ehret, the then-owner. Extensive alterations were made and the rooms were fitted out in the spirit of the early American overseas trade. Mr. Straight donated the Chinese art objects, and Mr. James A. Farrell, the President, gave, then and later, rare ship models, engravings, and pictures of Asiatic countries and leaders of American commerce. Mrs. Straight presented the collection of thirty-five ship models and subsequently a large collection of paintings, prints, maritime relics, and other decorations which had been loaned to the Club when organized and had given it much of its unique atmosphere.

In 1918 Willard Straight bought the property with the idea that India House might someday wish to own it. Through the generosity of Mrs. Straight, now Mrs. Leonard K. Elmhirst, the India House group acquired the place at a very reasonable figure in February 1921, and on the expiration of certain leases in 1924, rearranged and rebuilt the interior, creating, through the work of Mr. W. A. Delano, the architect, what is now known as the Marine Room, famous for its charm, beauty and English club atmosphere.

If the doorman is in the mood, he may show the house to you. Ordinarily, the club is open only to members and their friends.

Five

Al Smith's Alma Mater

EAST THIRD STREET

FULTON MARKET, Alfred E. Smith's college, is a rough and ready school. Wet pavements, shouting hucksters, and the smell of fish make a hurly-burly, but picturesque scene, little changed since 1822, the date of its birth.

The best time to visit the Fulton Fish Market is early in the morning; it opens at six. If you can stand the smell, the market is fascinating. Your nose will guide you to it. Strange eels, seahorses, and other denizens of the deep fill the stalls.

We poked around the marketplace and inspected some of the boats tied at anchor off the docks across the way. They were fishing smacks, many from a great distance. The majority are, however, New England sailing vessels. The bluefish are hooked off Newport. The flounder comes from Long Island Sound and the swordfish are caught near Montauk Point. Lobsters are Maine products. The oysters come from Maryland and the terrapin from around Baltimore. One of the most unique characters of the Fulton Fish Market is Moore, the terrapin man. His coaling station is on Front Street. He keeps the terrapin in great drawers, on their backs. They are bought on the hook, as it were, like lobsters. To ensure their freshness, they are sold alive. Green turtles and terrapins come to thirty cents a pound. Mr. Moore has the greatest assortment in New York. He has been in business for forty years. He supplies banquets, private parties, and the more fashionable clubs. Mrs. Steinway buys her Christmas terrapin off him.

About the first market established in New York, was one that dealt in fish. It stood at the foot of Coenties Slip in 1664. Later it moved to Burling Slip, and finally, in 1822, landed in the east wing of the new city market at Fulton Street.

I guess the produce and meat dealers objected to the smell of fish, for in 1830, we find a petition entered in the City Council, for the erection of a building to be used only for fish between Beekman and Fulton Streets on South. The petition was granted. The fish dealers congregated here until 1848 when a larger building replaced their old quarters. This stayed put until they began widening South Street in 1905. Plans were drawn up for a new market. On March 18, 1907, the fishermen moved into the present building. The market was now entirely theirs.

Wear rubbers when you visit the Fulton Fish Market. The sidewalks are always being flooded, to keep them clean. Thousands of fish are handled in the old stalls each day. Go down to the docks, as we did, and watch the mackerel being shoveled out by hundreds of men. See the ice chopped by the big machine at the edge of the wharf and look at the barrels, used for shipping the fish, as they are packed. The system is fascinating. Business is carried on in a big way.

After a morning in the Fulton Fish Market, Ruth Steinway and I decided that to be consistent we must lunch at Sweet's. We ordered fresh bluefish. It cost forty cents a portion. The old hotel looks much as it did when Philip Hone was mayor of New York in 1848.

The East River was a network of shipyards then. Mr. Hone writes in his famous diary of seeing the great vessel, the *New Netherlands*, launched from the shipyard at the head of Cherry Street, of being among those present when the *Liverpool*, a noble packet, was launched by Bell & Brown at the foot of Houston Street, and of visiting Sullivan's Shipyards between Eighth and Ninth Streets also along the East River.

The portions at Sweet's are abundant. Go early. The place is crowded with businessmen of the district as well as sailors.

Sullivan's Shipyards, of which Mr. Hone speaks, are still in existence. We wandered through them. There is a nice fragrance of wood in the air. Great spars lie on the ground. The offices savor of the past.

If you are interested in articles of a nautical flavor, stop as we did at the Alfred Moch Ship Supply Shop on the waterfront at 36 South Street. Mrs. Steinway bought a pair of brass lamp lanterns for her summer cottage in New England here, paying three dollars and fifty cents for them. The day we wandered into this shop two great silver eagles were poised on top of coils of rope.

"Where did they come from?" we asked.

"Oh, those were on the old Iron Steamboats," the proprietor said. "We've been renting them for fifteen dollars a month to the Paramount movie people. The pair are worth sixty dollars apiece."

THE LIGHT OF OTHER DAYS,
'A SHIP CHANDLER'S SHOP'

They were beautifully carved birds done after the fashion of the figureheads that once decorated the clipper ships and probably by the same type of artist who also carved cigar-store Indians.

We turned a bit off the riverfront to find that Indian. It stood in front of a snuff shop at 396 Water Street. This emblem of snuff and tobacco, so common a few years ago, has become the target for collectors. Their scarcity as well as their rough but sometimes good hand-carving make them valuable.

The men who sculpted figureheads for clipper ships included tobacco-shop figures. Many of these artists lived on South Street in the old houses we passed.

I am inclined to believe that the Indian outside Paul Lavalle's tobacco shop was carved by neighborhood talent. An old lady who used to run the store owned it up to the day she died in February of the year nineteen thirty-three.

To her knowledge, it was eighty years old. She had lived in the district all of her life.

Though her son has sold the shop, he permits the present owners to keep the Indian. But he is very fond of it and guards it carefully. If you examine it closely, you will see that it is well anchored to the store with heavy wiring.

"That is because some of the boys over at the Journal offices carried it off one night to a speak-easy," Paul Lavalle said. "We got it back, but we've tied it down since then." The Hearst newspaper offices at 210 South Street back up on Water Street.

Strangely in contrast to the old-fashioned naivete of the wooden Indian, is the sinister market which drifts into being each day beneath the arches of the Manhattan Bridge just a few blocks away at Cherry and South Streets.

The men bring odds and ends of everything to sell or trade. One shoe, an old bottle, a piece of curtain, and half a straw hat, are worth a good hour's bartering. Sometimes they display bits of jewelry. No questions are asked.

"Do you believe in Jesus Christ?" A man thrust a cheap

reproduction of The Last Supper under our noses. "How'd you like to buy this for ten cents?" he snarled.

Religion of the camp-meeting variety covers the waterfront. Every fifth house is a mission. Scandinavian, Baptist, Methodist —they elbow one another with huge signs marked "Christ Will Save," "Come to Jesus" and "Forsake the Devil for the Lord."

Mrs. Steinway and I stopped in one of the missions. It was on the corner of James Slip and South Street. The house that sheltered it must have been more than a century old. Rickety wooden steps led to the entrance. It was spotlessly clean. The floors had been scrubbed until they were white.

A man let us in.

"I be a Swedish sailor," he said in broken English. "I came into Jesus when I was sick. Bayne here since."

He had the simple face of a child. Revivals, he told us, were held at seven o'clock on Tuesday and Thursday nights.

Our next call was at a tiny place tucked back in a maze of lilac bushes. The fragrant lavender flowers were budding when we stopped in front of Hannah Murray's home that May morning. It, too, like the wooden Indian, faced Front Street just back of the river highway.

"Yes, she lived here all her life," said a pleasant-faced woman who leaned out of an upper window to answer our inquiry about the owner of the old house. "She died not long ago. I am her daughter. She was eighty-one years old."

A quaint picket fence guarded the place, a plantain tree shaded it. A flagged walk led to the front door. The house was frame with tiny-paned windows. The roof sagged pathetically.

"Poor house, it's sort of going to pieces since Mother went,"

Hannah Murray's daughter said. "She loved it. Sometimes I think houses are like people. They live just so long. Now that Mother's gone, it feels it hasn't much reason for staying on. My children think it's too old-fashioned.

" 'Gee, Ma!' they say, 'why do we have to live in a house that has a shed and a cellar door in the front yard?'"

A book to do with the waterfront must necessarily touch not only upon the docks, the ships, and the people concerned with it, but also upon the implements known to mariners.

Though the sailmakers and rope-workers have faded like snarks out of the picture, there are a few marine supply shops still in existence on the waterfront.

The most celebrated is the Negus Brothers of 69 Pearl Street. They deal in anything and everything pertaining to boats.

But there is one thing that even the Negus boys haven't got in stock, and that's an astrolabe. Samuel Verplanck Hoffman, whose ancestors owned a country estate on the East River, has cornered the market on astrolabes. People don't run across them every day of the week. Mr. Hoffman's collection is the largest in the country.

The nearest thing to an astrolabe is the ancient French sextant that belongs to Captain Robert Huntington, principal of the Merchant Marine School at the Seamen's Institute.

"It was difficult to find anything out about astrolabes," Mr. Hoffman said, in his offices at 258 Broadway. "Nobody seemed to have made a record of them. I asked a professor of English at Johns Hopkins one day if he had ever heard of any books on astrolabes. He laughed, and said, 'Yes. Chaucer wrote a good deal on the subject. He explained, to his nephew, in a lengthy treatise, the geometrical principles involving the working of astrolabes.'

"I really discovered more about them through Chaucer," continued Mr. Hoffman, "than any other person. You've got to know quite a bit about the stars, to understand them, however."

Mr. Hoffman is a meticulous soul. His beloved astrolabes are neatly numbered and carefully stowed away in a big safe set in one of the many rooms given over to the Hoffman estate on the fifth floor of the office building at the corner of Broadway and Warren Street.

"So many rooms," I said, "how do you ever fill them?"

Mr. Hoffman smiled. "With relatives. Sometimes when we have board meetings, I don't think they're big enough."

The Hoffman family is so closely linked with the early history of New York and the waterfront that I feel it must be part of this book.

Matilda Hoffman whose name ancient gossips linked with that of Washington Irving, is an ancestor of Samuel Verplanck Hoffman.

"They say she was engaged to Irving," he said, stroking his neatly pointed white beard. "But nobody has ever proved it. There's been much controversy over the matter."

Whenever Irving went to call on Matilda Hoffman, he sailed in a sloop up the East River, docking at her father's estate near the Gracie Mansion.

The celebrated Hoffman House, once the fashionable hotel of New York, was named after Mr. Hoffman's grandmother.

"She owned the two lots upon which it was built," he explained, eying an astrolabe, as he spoke. They are first, and his family second, with the man who is a descendant of New York's most distinguished East River settlers.

Six

Clipper Ship Ghosts

GRAND old ghosts, they are, these spirits of the packet boats. Memories of their runs linger in the minds of Corlear's Hook Park early settlers.

Many of the people who live in the delightful old houses that nestle in the side streets near the water are descendants of the sailing captains who skippered wind-jammers.

Take John Taylor, for instance, a neighbor of Hannah Murray's; our second walk ended at his house. He has passed his entire life on the waterfront. From the sitting-room window of his little house on Front Street, he can watch the docks, where in days gone by, great clipper ships, such as his father skippered, sailed into port.

These picturesque wind-jammers went to every part of the world, bringing back with them the flavor of far-off countries. John Taylor recalls hearing his father talk of Griswold, the China

House, Hoyt and Tom, the celebrated East India firm, and Thomas H. Smith and Sons, the Great South Street merchants.

Thomas Smith owned an enormous tea shop on South Street near Dover. It extended through to Water Street and was the wonder of the city when it was built. The dock near it was named India Wharf. Up to 1834, the cargo of the East India boats landing at South Street was principally tea. Later articles designed in Paris were sent to China to be duplicated at a tenth of the cost and then brought here to be sold. Among the first great sailing vessels to carry this new cargo to the South Street merchants were the *Howard*, the *Tomulus*, and the *Thomas Dickinson*. The ships usually made the passage to China in ninety-seven days and returned in ninety.

Because of the imitative qualities of the Chinese and the cheap cost of labor, New York in the 'forties was flooded with Chinese-made goods, such as fireworks, joss sticks, lacquer fans, horn forks and knives, feather fans, checkered matting, and brilliant silks. It is easy to picture the riot of color the great white-sailed ships must have poured onto the gray docks that John Taylor now stares at from his lattice-paned sitting-room window.

South Street has other ghosts than the clipper ships. The great East India merchants of the waterfront are characters to be reckoned with. There was old John A. Moore, who had a large store on the corner of Water Street and Old Slip, a sturdy, stubby little man, with fiery red hair and a round freckled face.

Neighbors of his were John and Isaac Delaplaine, who owned a counting house in the same block, and the not-to-be-forgotten William Walton, founder of the Marine Society of New York, who died the early part of the nineteenth century.

The Waltons were one of New York's great families. No water-front book is complete that does not mention their names. The first of the names was Robert Walton, who had his shipyards as late as 1728 near what is now Peck Slip.

The Walton house at 328 Pearl Street boasted a garden that touched the river. Then the water came up to what is now Water Street. From Peck Slip up to Roosevelt were the shipyards. The first in this neighborhood was Mr. Roosevelt's—next came Walton and last VanHorn. Benjamin Peck was on the south side of the Slip.

The wharf at this point bore Walton's name. William Walton's house was Exhibit A in old New York. Great entertainments were given at his home. A descendant of the Waltons, Major T. J. Oakley Rhinelander, has a picture of the Walton mansion in his office on Williams Street. The square riggers and sloops that Walton owned brought him vast wealth. Practically all of the early ships sailing from New York docks were built in his shipyard.

Some of the Waltons lived on Front Street, John Taylor's neighborhood. Mrs. Abraham Walton made her home after her husband died, at 269 Water Street, in the block back of Front Street. The Waltons were very proud and haughty people.

A few of the houses that they must have known, linger on Front Street. Many are sagging, with windows broken and roofs rotting, others have been kept in repair.

Mrs. Steinway and I stopped at a nicely painted, red-brick Colonial house two doors below John Taylor's. A cheerful Italian woman and her husband, a truck driver, owned it. They had worked hard to keep it in good condition. It was amusing to find Italian peasant taste cropping out in the many-colored tiled floors, flowered wallpaper, and fringed counterpanes. At any rate, the effect was clean and neat, and the woman proud of it.

Little change had been made in John Taylor's house. I am sure that the same furnishings, wallpaper, and paint that his father selected, had been left untouched. There was even a rural air to the backyard, which featured not only a porch and wood shed but a chicken yard.

Contemporary with John Taylor is Jack Coagly who lives on the corner of South and Jackson Streets, in the cold-water walk-up tenement with the straggling row of stores strung beneath it. Mr. Coagly is a pioneer diver. The river beds surrounding Manhattan Island are an open book to him.

"How many times have I been down?" He shook his head. "Shucks I ain't kept count."

In appearance, he suggests a weather-beaten rock with barnacles of age clinging to it. He forgets when he was born, remembers nothing but the water and Corlear's Hook Park, and smiles when asked about the romance of diving.

"It just takes a little nerve," he said. "There ain't no excitement to it."

He thinks that it was long in the 'nineties that he first went down.

"Diving was an individual matter then," he said, "now it's a corporation business. The small fellows have been froze out."

A diving suit costs anywhere from eight hundred dollars to seventeen hundred dollars. Mr. Coagly owned six, together with his partner, Walsh. He has gone down for everything from human bodies to sunken ships.

"What about pirate gold?" I asked, "have you ever found any?"

"Naw, lady, it would cost more to take it anyway, than it would to leave it lay."

"Why?"

"The Underwriters. They want everything."

The deepest hole around Manhattan Island is off Blackwell's Island. "It is one hundred and ten feet deep," said Mr. Coagly. "Many the time I've been in it."

"What did you see down there?"

"Fish. Curious fellows. Some are pretty big."

But he does no diving now. Though endowed with the office of deputy sheriff, he sits for the most part in his little corner room and watches the waters he once explored.

Sometimes a four-masted schooner drifts by. "But not often," said Mr. Coagly, "they're back numbers."

I saw one the day I called on Mr. Coagly. The afternoon was misty. A fog hung over the East River. Suddenly out of the white haze, the ghostly specter of a clipper loomed up, with sails furled. Its great spars, high prow, and low sides duplicated the pictures of the old wind jammers that once lined South Street. Like some haunted derelict, it drifted down the bay. As we watched it, the boat vanished into the fog.

Seven

A Murder Stable

A THUNDER shower drove us into the murder stable. We passed it on our way to the East River from Third Avenue at the start of our second walk. We were hurrying along Allen Street when the storm came up. It was a spectacular shower with great flashes of lightning, a roar of thunder, and a heavy down-pour to make it terrifying.

"Goodness!" we cried; "let's get out of this." The day was warm. We had on thin dresses. We shared an umbrella. With the rain pelting us we dashed into the nearest shelter. It was a dark and gloomy stable. Not a soul was in sight. We stood for a few minutes watching the storm and shaking the water from our frocks. The steady slanting lines gave no promise of letting up.

"I'm afraid we'll have to stay here for a little while," Mrs. Steinway said. We looked about. By this time our eyes were accustomed to the dim light of the musty old building. It was dark lonely and silent. We shivered a little. And then we stared at each other.

"What is the number of this place?" Ruth Steinway asked.

I peeked out.

"Fifty-nine Allen Street," I said slowly. "This is the stable where Mr. Ridley and his secretary were murdered!"

Curiosity overcame our fear. We searched around for an office. Flashes of lightning revealed it. A man dozing in a chair with five or six kittens playing about him started up as we stepped in.

"Yes, this is where Ridley was murdered," he said. "Could I show you his office?" He hesitated.

"This is the first day a policeman hasn't been on guard. Well, I guess I might take you down."

Timidly we followed him to the rickety elevator. "Who am I? My name is Joseph Fiduccia. I am the man who found Ridley and his secretary lying dead on the floor in his sub-cellar. Me and my brother rented this stable off him."

Mr. Fiduccia liked Mr. Ridley. "Why didn't they take his money without killing him?" he asked. "Poor old man, he never bothered anybody. They say he was tight-fisted. Well, why shouldn't he be? It was his own money."

We trailed Joseph Fiduccia to the sub-cellar, riding down to it in an ancient elevator of the rope-pulling type.

A flash light guided us. Mr. Ridley's offices were two floors beneath the street level. The chill of the tomb was upon them.

"There's where I found him," Joseph Fiduccia said, pointing to a corner littered with papers. "His secretary lay near."

Fifty years ago Ridley's Department Store was the fashionable shop of New York. It fronted on Grand Street. Two thousand people were employed by the old man murdered the May of 1933 in the dank sub-cellar stable. His department store is a thing of the past. Ridley stepped out of it with a huge fortune. He lived the life of a hermit. His comings and goings were a mystery to East-Side neighbors, but he continued to retain his connection with the locality by keeping a rabbit-warren office in the sub-cellar of the former Ridley stables.

"Many is the time I have tried to get him up in my offices," mourned Joseph Fiduccia. "But he wouldn't budge out of this cellar."

The Ridley murder is one of the unsolved mysteries of New York. The dead secretary, Lee Weinstein, was said to be an accomplice of two accountants, who confessed to plotting the robbing of Ridley's estate. They were sent to Sing Sing.

The theory is that Ridley was killed in trying to save his secretary who was evidently shot first.

The Ridley stables are now in the heart of the brass shop district of New York. Five out of six stores on this street shadowed by the elevated deal in brass and copper. Contemporary with Mr. Ridley is Mrs. John Heins' little frame house on East Fourth Street.

On our way from East Street to Exterior, or Marginal, we touched Lewis Street, a tiny thoroughfare. This neighborhood missed those two bankers, J. P. Morgan and Charlie Mitchell, when they didn't show up last spring.

There are no traffic lights on Lewis Street. It runs from Grand to Eighth, parallel with the waterfront. Because of this and because of the fact that it forms a connecting link with Wall Street, the two financiers traversed it daily, until they were called to Washington by the Congressional Investigating Committee.

Morgan rode in an old-fashioned Rolls-Royce. "One of them high-bodied-things," said George Heins, proprietor of the restaurant at 395 East Fourth Street. We had stopped at his eating place for a sandwich. "We could set the clock by his passing," he continued, "never varied in the time."

Mr. Mitchell wasn't so regular. "He was liable to shoot by any minute in any kind of a car," Mr. Heins said. "Sometimes it would be one of these affairs that shut the driver out and again it might be a flivver."

Heins paused to flick a few crumbs off the table with his dish towel. "You know, when them fellows don't drive through, there's something empty about the street. We all got to watching for them each day. I'd be slicin' cheese or ham, and I'd look out the window and see that old Rolls-Royce, and I'd say, 'Gee, Morgan's running on schedule, all right.' Or I'd hear a lot of tootin' of horns and I'd stick my head through the door to see what all the shoutin' was about and I'd see Mitchell."

"How'd I know him? Well, I got a relative that works down in the National City Bank. He pointed him out to me one time. And then he told me to watch for Charlie Mitchell along Lewis Street, said that was the way he always drove to the bank."

George and his twin brother, Theodore, run the old-fashioned eating place on the corner of Fourth and Lewis Streets. Their name has been on the window since 1859 when the great-uncle of these boys hung out the sign bearing the legend, "Heins' Restaurant."

Then the vast shipyards along the waterfront furnished patrons. There was John Roach, maker of the finest square riggers afloat and builder of the first fire-proof office structure in New York; Philip Hone's friend who owned the big shipyard at the foot of Cherry Street;

Messrs. Bell and Brown, proprietors of the large shipyard at the foot of Houston Street, and Mr. John Sullivan, owner of the great shipyard at the foot of East Ninth Street, the only yard now in existence.

William Munzer is the superintendent of Sullivan's Shipyard. He's been with the firm for thirty-three years.

Known originally as the John W. Sullivan's Shipyard Works, it is now being run by Mr. Sullivan's sons, Fred B., Harrison M., and Irving L. Sullivan. When the old yard first went into commission, the shingle was hung out on Water Street; from there it moved to South Street, and now it occupies the former John L. Roach Shipyard at the foot of East Ninth Street.

To-day the company specializes in tug, ferry and steamboats. Clipper ships and square riggers are ghosts of the past.

Heins' restaurant is homey. There is one big long table in the room back of the bar about which everyone sits. It faces the huge coal stove where the meals are cooked.

The Heins twins were born in the little yellow-frame house that adjoins the restaurant. It is about one hundred and fifty years old. Mrs. Heins came there as a bride.

They say the house was built by a ship's carpenter who worked in one of the nearby yards. We liked the lumber as well as the shipyards in this neighborhood. There is the fragrance of cedar and white pine over the district and the leisurely atmosphere of other days. Great spars of mahogany and cedar lie in Sullivan's Yard, spars and masts with enough give and strength to withstand the heaviest sail and stiffest wind.

Our third waterfront trip led us far inland. We set out to explore the Harlem shoreline and wound up in a crowded tenement district on East Third Street.

The reason for the deflection of our course, was S. Klein, the dress man on Union Square. Mrs. Steinway had been eager to meet him because he purchased the old Steinway Hall on East Fifteenth Street for an annex to his store on Union Square. The famous auditorium is now used for the cloak and suit business.

Surrounded by aldermen, policemen, and members of The Cooper Union Council, the little man, whose success story reads like an Horatio Alger novel, beamed as an amiable Billikin might, when we met him at an East Third Street playground one warm June afternoon.

He was among a group that was presenting the playground to the neighborhood. He came bustling forward, waving his hands at the crowds of comfortably proportioned mamas, papas, and children. "These are my people!" he cried. They cheered. Speeches were made, and pictures taken.

Fairly bursting with excitement, Klein finally left his playground. He nodded at the old tenements, the overflowing fire escapes, and the narrow streets. "This is my neighborhood," he explained to us.

"Where did you live?" Mrs. Steinway asked.

"At 78 Eldridge Street," he answered. "Four blocks from the East River. I was five years old when we came here from Russia."

"What about looking at the house?" I suggested. Klein interested me as a character. Eldridge Street is a thoroughfare of rear house tenements, peopled by sweat-shop workers. The buildings cover ground once occupied by the Colonial landowners whose estates stretched to the East River.

The June afternoon of our visit, the heat had driven the people into the streets. Old and young swarmed steps and curbs. Sitting in front of Number 78 was a very ancient, stoop-shouldered, little white-haired woman.

Mr. Klein spoke to her in Yiddish. "She has lived here thirty-eight years," he said. "She remembers my mother. Her name is Mrs. Cohen."

Together they gossiped about changes in the house. Though she said she recalled Mrs. Klein, the name meant nothing to her. She spoke of her son in Denver and handed us a letter from him to read. "He is a very good boy," she said, "but he is sick. He has consumption. He sends me two dollars a week to live on."

As we left Mr. Klein reached in his pocket and pulled out a twenty-dollar bill. He put it in Mrs. Cohen's hand.

"It's from an old neighbor," he said.

Eight

The Dark Side

GRIM, soot-streaked brick walls, towering black smoke-stacks, gaunt buildings, and lonely blocks stretched ahead of us on our jaunt up Lewis Street from Fourth to Fourteenth, along the East River. Coal yards, power plants, city dumping docks and abandoned piers separated us from the waterfront as we were forced even farther inland at Avenue D. The New York Edison Power Station formed an impasse at Fourteenth Street. Pittsburgh at its worst could not have been more Mephistophelian than the East River shore at this point.

The one interesting spot was a boat-shaped gray building on the south side of Fourteenth Street, not far from Avenue D. It is occupied by the offices of the Eagle Pencil Company. We stepped in to inquire about the history of the old structure. The black marble mantelpieces and walnut woodwork dated it in the 'sixties.

"Our Mr. Berwald can tell you the story," said a clerk. "Ask for him at the general information bureau, just around the corner at 630 East Thirteenth Street."

"It is the first fire-proof office building put up in New York," A. H. Berwald said. "John Roach, the shipyard man, designed it. The windows were originally portholes. He wanted it to look like a boat. You'll find a good many seafaring things around this part of the waterfront, but you'll lose all that when you get farther up."

Our path from the Eagle Pencil Company led up Avenue D. It was not until we reached Exterior Street, that we were again on the riverfront. Avenue D is in the heart of the slums. Fire escapes overflow with bedding and garbage. Snide little organizations meet in empty stores. "Social Clubs," the signs on the doors say. "Gangsters," the police say.

Exterior has a way of changing its name. Just now it is Marginal. There has been talk of continuing it down to South Ferry. It extends from Seventeenth Street to Twenty-Fourth, on the East River. With hopeful steps, we turned into it. The way in the few blocks preceding had smudged our faces and dampened our spirits. Huge stacks belched forth black smoke above us. Gray buildings shut out our view of the water.

We were hedged in by a miniature inferno of power plants and city dumping vats. To turn suddenly from this into a fresh, clean open space was heaven.

Exterior or Marginal Street is famous for its Sunday baseball games. The kids of the neighborhood come here to play. There is little traffic during the week-end. This locality has known life. It was much used in days gone by because of the ferry that paddled to Greenpoint. However, though it still runs, there is little need of the boat. Sometimes an occasional motorist makes use of it, for a shortcut to Long Island.

Alongside the ferry house at Twenty-Fourth Street, the *Macom*, official greeter's yacht during Jimmie Walker's regime as Mayor of the City of New York, swings at anchor. More celebrities have steamed up the bay on this boat, than any other craft of its size in the world, they say. It is a comfortable thing, on the order of a glorified tug. Grover Whalen heads the record for the number of trips made on it.

Another landmark of the locality is the Society for the Prevention of Cruelty to Animals. Its headquarters are in that big white building on the corner of Twenty-Fourth Street and Avenue A.

It is amazingly well equipped, with various types of ambulances, operating rooms, and animal refuges. One of the ambulances is large enough to carry an elephant. It is sometimes used when the circus comes to town. People often pension their pets by boarding them at the Society Sanitarium.

Bess, Julia Morisini's favorite horse, was brought here when Miss Morisini died. She left word in her will that a certain sum of money was to be set aside to pay for Bess's board at the S. P. C. A. Her father was a partner of Jay Gould, the great Wall Street speculator and one of the first stockholders in the New York Elevated Railway.

The Twenty-Fourth Street ferry section marked the end of

our second walk. We rested a while on the docks before we called it a day.

There is a fascination about sitting on these old wooden piers which line the waterfront. Nova Scotia and New England traffic was making its way up the East River, that June afternoon. It was close on to six o'clock. The *Commonwealth* of the Fall River Line, white-bodied, black-smoke-stacked, steamed by. A Nova Scotia lumber schooner, with auxiliary engines chugging, moved slowly past our dock. These old boats represent the last stand of sailing vessels. Sight of them on a windy day, when with all sails hoisted they move up the Sound, gives one a meager idea of what local waters must have looked like, when every craft afloat was a square rigger.

The majority of the Nova Scotia boats anchor off City Island. A few venture farther down. In sharp contrast to the romantic lines of the Nova Scotian lumber vessels were the solid, matter-of-fact yellow brick Municipal bath buildings a few hundred yards up the riverfront.

The high point of Greenpoint Ferry history was touched when James Hazen Hyde enjoyed a summer residence at Greenpoint, in the early part of the twentieth century.

The front-page executive of the Equitable Life Insurance Company entertained, they say, the King of Abyssinia, or some such potentate, on his Greenpoint estate, and embarked, they say, with the visiting ruler, from the docks at the foot of East Twenty-Third Street, on a specially chartered boat.

A glamourous touch, that Hyde expedition, to this seemingly drab neighborhood.

Nine

The Largest Bedroom in the World

CLIFF-SHACK
BELOW GRANT'S TOMB

AT THE foot of East Twenty-Fifth Street, on a pier, is New York's biggest bedroom. Seventeen hundred and fifty men sleep in it every night. It is called Annex Number One. The pier belongs to the Municipal Lodging House at East Twenty-Fifth Street and the river. Counting the main building, this pier, and Annex Number Two at the foot of Whitehall Street, forty-five hundred men and women a night are given shelter.

The street that leads to the Lodging House is lonely. Uneven pavements and grimy red-brick buildings add to its gloom.

On stormy days ragged men and women stand in the doorways and lean against walls. They are waiting to get into the Lodging House. Though the line forms, in wet weather, early in the afternoon, the doors are not opened until five—unless the storm is very bad.

However, from then on, the homeless men and women are sure of a hot meal, bath, and bed. We missed the Municipal Lodging House, the June morning we began our third walk up First Avenue. But we went back one cold snowy afternoon in December to look it over. Already a few stragglers were in the street. Some of the older men had been taken inside. They sat patiently in a little anteroom.

As a rule, J. A. Mannis, the superintendent, doesn't let them stay in the day-time, because the place has to be made clean for the night. Every morning, it is scrubbed from top to bottom, fresh linen put on the beds, blankets fumigated, and food made ready for the evening meal.

Few questions are asked first-time applicants come. If they return, they are sent back to the Central Registration Bureau at South Ferry to file their names, in case of accident or death.

All types drift in. Before the depression, the men were mostly of the laboring class, and the women, houseworkers. After 1929, however, skilled mechanics, stenographers, and college women turned up. One man came who had lost one hundred thousand dollars in Wall Street. He slept two nights in the Lodging House. He is back in the Street now.

Though women are never turned away, Mr. Mannis does not like to see them.

"This is no place for the average woman," he said. "Not

because of the surroundings, but because of other women. The majority that we do get are pretty tough. If any of the better class come, it is hard for them."

The women's dormitory is on the second floor of the main building. It has windows on three sides, is light and airy, and overlooks the rooftops of a few adjoining sheds, as well as the East River. There are one and two-tier beds and a small corner for cribs for those with children.

The dormitory for the men is on the third floor. Here, the beds are all double-deckers.

Before the lodgers can eat, they have to take a bath and be examined by a physician. When they are ready to go to bed, fresh night shirts are handed to them and their own clothing put in the steam room to be fumigated. The evening meal consists of good hot stew, four slices of bread and a cup of coffee. For breakfast, they get cereal and milk, coffee, and fruit.

Those who wish may spend the day in Cheer Lodge at 630 East Sixth Street, where their clothes can be mended and pressed. If the men want it, they can get a shave.

On Thanksgiving and Christmas, Mr. Mannis hands out turkey or chicken with all the trimmings no questions asked. In 1932, he had a run on his dinners. Ten thousand came. He didn't have enough to go around. On Thanksgiving of the following year, he prepared ten thousand dinners and had only fifty-two hundred guests turn up. Some of these were repeaters.

"Which all goes to show," he said, "that conditions are better. I notice it too, in the type of men and women we get. A year ago, they were young. Now fifty-five percent, are over fifty."

Mr. Mannis gave us these statistics: The present main

Municipal Lodging House, erected in 1908 and officially opened in 1909, is located at 432 East Twenty-Fifth Street in the Borough of Manhattan. Seven stories in height, it has a capacity of 903 beds, providing accommodations for 651 male lodgers, 152 female lodgers, 6 children, and 94 employees; a total of 903. The clothing sterilization plant has a capacity of 320 suits an hour.

The accommodations for women, which comprise the entire second floor, include besides the dormitory and dining room, a sitting room with piano, radio, a sewing machine, baths, and a small laundry. In addition, private rooms are provided for men and women employees, an office for the house physician, a medical clinic for men and women, recreation rooms, library and a tailor shop.

Annex Number One, which is located at the foot of East Twenty-Fifth Street, was opened on November 22, 1930, and has accommodations for 1529 lodgers with complete kitchen facilities as well as facilities for 143 employees.

In the latter part of 1930, it became obvious that additional facilities would be required to take care of the rapidly increasing number of applicants for lodgings, and on March first Annex Number Two in the Thirty-Ninth Street Brooklyn Ferry Terminal at the foot of Whitehall Street, Borough of Manhattan, was opened with complete lodging-house facilities and a bed capacity which now provides for 1850 lodgers and 98 employees.

One of the greatest handicaps New York has had to face during the whole of the present depression has been the tremendous influx of the unemployed of other communities. Many of these were industrious, hard-working persons whose presence, should they elect to stay, would reflect credit upon the town. Others, such as will be found in all communities, were tatterdemalions who had no desire to work but preferred to eke out an existence on city streets, by approaching pedestrians for a small pittance. To cope with the undesirable situation created by this latter element, and for the purpose of securing complete centralized control over all homeless persons of New York, the Central Registration Bureau for the Homeless was opened on the site of the Municipal Lodging House, Annex Number Two, at the Thirty-Ninth Street Brooklyn Ferry Terminal, foot of Whitehall Street, Manhattan, on October 1, 1931.

The Bureau was established and operated by the Welfare Council of New York City in cooperation with the Municipal Lodging House of this Department and other agencies caring for the homeless. Through a system of centralized registration outlined in more detail in the Municipal Lodging House section of this report, applicants for food and shelter were given registration cards by the Central Registration Bureau and assigned to the Municipal Lodging House or other agencies, dependent upon the length of residence of the applicant in the city and other facts involved. While residents found to be temporarily in need of food and shelter were admitted to the Municipal Lodging House as often as circumstances required, the rule of one night a month for non-residents was still applied, and after the latter were taken care of they were referred back to the Central Registration Bureau where they were assigned to some other agency which was not concerned with the residency phase of the question.

The public was requested through the press and by the radio to withhold contributions to those approaching them on the streets for money to secure food and shelter and to refer them instead, to the Central Registration Bureau to be cared for as aforementioned. This Bureau fills a long-felt want. As a result of its establishment, the method of caring for the homeless now ranks with the best obtaining in any form of organized relief in the City of New York.

During 1931, the Municipal Lodging House furnished 889,984 lodgings and 2,668,226 meals which, with the attendant sterilization of clothing, baths, physical examinations, etc., is what may rightfully be termed a "Herculean" task. Bellevue, the city's hospital which extends from East Twenty-Sixth Street to Twenty-Ninth Street, is a neighbor of the Lodging House.

The poor of New York mill in and out of the great drab buildings in a vast torrential flood of humanity.

The smell of an institution hangs like a pall over the neighborhood. Day and night the clanging of ambulance bells is in the air. Twenty-two hundred people a day pour through the crowded corridors of Bellevue at Twenty-Sixth Street and the East River. Seven hundred a week lie on the marble slabs of the city morgue at East Twenty-Seventh Street and the waterfront. As many are carried four times a month to Hart's Island aboard the "Last Ferry," the wheezy little tug that anchors off the now demolished recreation pier at the foot of East Twenty-Sixth Street. Here it was that the victims of the *Slocum* disaster were brought on that July day in 1904 when the Lutheran excursion boat sank off Blackwell's Island.

We entered Bellevue through the Twenty-Sixth Street entrance, stepping into the one old building that is still standing on this street. Visitors use this entrance and also the reporters from various papers who have an office to the left of the main waiting room.

The back door leads into the court, where the first buildings of Bellevue cluster. To the right is the long wood-covered passageway that once led to the alcoholic ward. Since the new wings have been added, I believe that this section is now used for administration purposes.

To the left of the court is a gray stone, Civil War-type of building that boasts a lovely old iron balcony. They say it is the balcony upon which Washington leaned when he took his oath of office as President of the United States. A winding stair leads to the little porch it trims. For many years, the general admission rooms were in this old building.

By cutting across the court and following the main passageway through the hospital, it is possible, to come out on Twenty-Seventh Street. Bellevue buildings extend on through to Twenty-Ninth Street; this includes the morgue, the new psychiatric wing, and the State Medical Examiner's offices, which is where the coroner does business.

Bellevue flanks the East River. It is impossible to follow the waterfront from Twenty-Fourth Street to Sutton Place. Where the City Welfare docks end at Twenty-Ninth Street, slaughterhouses, tenements, and fashionable apartment houses prevented us from keeping to the shoreline.

First Avenue was necessarily our only highway. A grim path at the start, bordered by towering slaughterhouses, dreary tenements, and peopled by poverty-stricken men, women, and children.

But First Avenue, like many other sections of New York, is a neighborhood of contrasts.

Ten

❧

Power and Packing Plants

OLD SHOT TOWER WHICH ONCE STOOD ON THE EAST RIVER BETWEEN 54TH AND 55TH STREET.

FROM Twenty-Sixth Street to Fifty-First, the way of our waterfront walk was as gray as the day.

We resented the mammoth power plants and packing houses that obliterated the shoreline. Seen from the outside, power plants are without romance. Their history, however, is rich in adventure. The great building with titanic smoke stacks at the foot of East Thirty-Fifth Street belongs to the New York Steam Service Company. It is known as the Kips Bay Station. It supplies heat to Rockefeller Center, the Empire State Building, and the new Grand Central Railway Station, as well as hundreds of other office structures in the district.

In the year that Thomas Edison appeared on the scene with

his electric lights and power companies, Wallace C. Andrews, a Cleveland financier, conceived the idea of heating New York by steam. In 1879, Mr. Edison and Mr. Andrews began tearing up city streets to lay their wires and pipes. Andrews had his followers. Mrs. Ulysses S. Grant was among the original stockholders in the steam company.

Though in nowise connected, Mr. Edison and Mr. Andrews often met in the survey of their work. Steam pipelines overlapped channels for wiring.

Today, they are near each other. The Kips Bay New York Steam plant is three blocks below the Edison Company's power station. In an arrangement, the latter supplies steam during the mornings of cold days to the former.

Thousands of mains form a network under the surface of Manhattan streets. Heat is sold by the pipe after the manner of water and gas.

The largest plant of the Corporation is the Kips Bay Station occupying an entire block on the East River between Thirty-Fifth and Thirty-Sixth Streets. It has a capacity of 2,450,000 pounds of steam an hour. Sufficient additional space is available for the enlargement of this station to a capacity of 7,000,000 pounds of steam an hour. Powdered bituminous coal is burned under the boilers which together with their equipment are of the most modern and efficient type. During the past year, one of the boilers generated the largest quantity of steam ever produced by a single boiler for a like period. The turbo-electric generators, used solely to provide energy for operating the auxiliary equipment in the station, have a capacity sufficient to supply the electric requirements of a small city. One of the seven coal pulverizing mills has a capacity of fifty tons an hour, substantially greater than any other similar mill in the world.

Next in importance is the Burling Slip Station, which is located near the financial district. This station was enlarged early in 1930 and now has a capacity of 1,800,000 pounds of steam an hour. It is one of the biggest and most efficient anthracite coal-burning steam plants in the country.

The Corporation also has two stations located at Fifty-Ninth and Sixtieth Streets on the East River, each having a capacity of 400,000 pounds of steam an hour. Their smokestacks flank the Queensborough Bridge. Only when workmen are digging the underground trenches in which the mains are to be laid may we catch a glimpse of the steel pipes through which the steam rushes at rates up to two hundred miles an hour. The forces to be controlled are appreciated when we see the massive pipes necessary to direct and confine the fluid over and under subways and car tracks; over, under, or around the many busy pipes, conduits, and other sub-surface structures; through tunnels of rock and concrete, and finally, to the consumer's door.

We walked out on the docks to see the huge plants at close range. We found strength in their ugliness and a fearful beauty in the white steam that hung, cloud-like, above the stacks.

A block below us, chugged the Thirty-Fourth Street ferry, a hang-over of the days when the Long Island had its terminal in Long Island City. Farther north, at Forty-Second Street, we could see the roofs of Tudor City, Fred French's real-estate development at the east end of a street, famous the world over.

Two historic spots lie on the waterfront in the fashionable East Fifties, the ground where Nathan Hale was executed, now covered by the Wilson slaughter-house at Forty-Sixth Street and First Avenue, and the site where the old Revolutionary shot tower stood at Fiftieth Street and the river.

A tablet on the Wilson building marks the location on which Nathan Hale was executed in September 1776. However, there is some dispute about this. Mrs. Steinway says that Felix Oldboy, in his Tour of Old New York, mentions Chambers Street as the site of the Hale gallows.

A dock rests above the shot-tower ground. This old landmark disappeared a comparatively few years ago. Gruenwald, the picture framer, told us that he recalled seeing it five years back. It was about three stories high and had an oven in it used originally for heating shot. It was put up, they say, during the Revolutionary War.

East River sailing sloops charted their course by it. Local residents used it as a guidepost for visiting friends. Felix Oldboy writes that they prefaced their remarks by such phrases as "You know where the old shot tower is."

Though the shot tower has gone to glory, Nathan Hale's tablet remains on the waterfront region to remind us of the early history of our island.

There is a sardonic touch to the fact that the slaughterhouse rises above the execution ground.

Government statistics show that New York ranks first and Chicago second in slaughterhouse figures. All of the Manhattan Island slaughterhouses lie on the waterfront.

The first ones Mrs. Steinway and I encountered on the East Side were at Forty-Sixth Street and First Avenue. They are in a neighborhood of contrasts; fringing them are the old slaughterhouse tenements, known in past police history as criminal rookeries. The slaughterhouse gangs were famed for their violence, fearlessness, and desperate character.

With the influx of high-priced apartment buildings, the tide has turned. The worst that can be said of the old houses today, is that they are cold-water tenements and as that class offer a doubtful shelter to the very poor.

There are three slaughterhouses in the First Avenue district. Sometimes a stray bull breaks away and tears up and down the highway. One charged the car of Speed Smylie a few years ago. Mr. Smylie, who is the head of the L. and S. Licorice Company, was living at the time on Gracie Square. First Avenue happened to be the highway he chose for the daily drive to his office. The bull was roped before he did any great damage to Mr. Smylie's automobile.

The big apartment buildings that flank the river at Turtle and Kip's Bay, prevented us from directly following the shoreline in this neighborhood. However, by turning off First Avenue at Forty-Ninth Street and walking through Mitchell Place to Beekman Place, we were enabled to stick pretty closely to the river's edge.

That huge tan brick apartment house at Three Mitchell Place is the Pan-Hellenic. It is the New York residence of the thousand-and-one sorority girls who come to town from various colleges throughout the country.

Mrs. A. Barton Hepburn is the guiding genius of it. Like the Junior League, the Pan-Hellenic provides not only living but recreation quarters for its tenants. There is a gymnasium, swimming pool, solarium, and ballroom as well as a restaurant and lecture hall.

Ruth Steinway and I didn't know it until we passed by, but later we learned that the Nathan Hale bronze tablet on the First Avenue side of the Wilson Packing Company was placed there in 1915 by a patriotic society to mark the spot where Nathan Hale was executed.

This packing plant at 816 First Avenue, was originally started under the name of Schwarzchild & Sulzberger many years ago. It was only a small plant then but has since grown until at present it covers the entire block between Forty-Fifth and Forty-Sixth Streets; that half fronting on Forty-Sixth Street takes in the big seven-story building with the killing beds (we didn't go in to see them; though people can), chill-rooms and sales coolers on the ground floor.

The meat is "Kosher killed." The firm caters to the Jewish religion, and everything comes under rabbinical inspection.

Wilson & Company was established by Ferdinand Sulzberger who later branched out and started a packing plant in Kansas City, as well as Chicago, where today the main offices are located, and from which the controlling interests of the firm operate.

The old company of Schwarzchild & Sulzberger was later changed to Sulzberger & Sons Co., the Schwarzchild interests leaving the company, but the old "S & S" name being maintained.

Later came the reorganization and the new name of "Wilson & Company" with Mr. Thomas E. Wilson as president. Today, not only does the company occupy this block, but it also runs modern smokehouses and refinery units in a large building on

Forty-Seventh Street, where tons of smoked meats are processed every year.

The building on Forty-Fifth and Forty-Sixth Streets, being operated for Jewish trade, does not handle any pork products except in a very small section set apart as the branch distributing room.

We were astonished to learn that the live cattle, sheep, and lambs are floated in cattle cars from Jersey and driven off of the boats directly into the plant where they are rested, fed, and watered until transferred to the killing floor.

These animals are then killed under the supervision of the Rabbis. Even after the animal is dressed, it is constantly under the eagle eyes of those bearded gentlemen. The various cuts and offal products are stamped or sealed by the Rabbis as proof and protection for the Jewish butcher.

The Packing House District is within waving distance of New York's Gold Coast!

We learned that the first packing house was established in the West in 1818 in Cincinnati. Prior to 1872, most of the slaughtering was done during the winter months. About that time chilling processes were developed and with the steady improvement in refrigeration began the rapid growth of the packing industry. Somewhere around 1878, this plant at First Avenue was erected.

Packing houses in the West kill and dress their own beef and small stock, also pork, and ship in refrigerated cars to distributing centers. Here in New York, there is one of these distributing centers at Thirty-Second Street and Twelfth Avenue, where Wilson & Company have opened up a branch house near the Hudson waterfront. Swift, Armour, and other packers are also represented in this market. Again, between Eleventh and Fourteenth Streets on Tenth Avenue there is another distributing center. There are not only meat products, but also poultry, produce, and so forth marketed.

The packing plants on the west shoreline of Manhattan Island are in the heart of the wholesale market district. Those we passed on the East Side were far removed from all thought of markets. Ahead of us loomed up the fashionable apartment buildings of the Beekman and Sutton Place section. Behind, straggled the gloomy institutions of charity.

As to the further details of Nathan Hale, the Revolutionary martyr, the First Avenue Association told us he spent the last night of his life in the Beekman greenhouse at Fifty-First Street and First Avenue. The greenhouse was part of one of the most beautiful estates on the East River.

The mansion lingered until 1874, a fine example of Colonial architecture. A fascinating web of historical legends was spun about it. Madame Riedesel, whose husband surrendered with Burgoyne, was responsible for many of the tales. Her characters were guests of the Beekmans.

But of course, the great episode was the trial of Nathan Hale, which took place in the drawing room. He was condemned to death by a group of British officers, within its four walls. Public School Number 135 stands on the site of the Beekman residence.

Into the kaleidoscopic pattern of First Avenue with its Nathan Hale background, fashionable apartment houses, slaughter-plants, power stations, and hospitals, is woven the thread of the spirit of Old First Avenue. It is kept upbroken, by the First Avenue Boys.

Whenever we stopped in any of the little stores, local restaurants or meeting places, the phrase "First Avenue Boys," was handed out to us.

"They know this neighborhood," the people said. "They can tell you anything you want to know."

Though we searched in vain for them on our walk from Twenty-Sixth Street, I finally tracked them down, several days later, by cornering John F. Turnier of 415 East Fifty-Eighth Street.

The First Avenue Boys, Inc., were organized for the purpose of "perpetuating the name, the traditions and ideals of First Avenue, and to promote the social, moral and civil welfare of its members." It was in the Hotel Ten Eyck at Albany that the plans were laid for the "Boys." A small group of East-Siders, including Commissioner Charlie Harnett, Martin McCue, the late Judge Max Levine, and several other political luminaries born near or on First Avenue, organized the association, in June of 1925. The first meeting was held in Terrace Garden. Among the famous members are Jimmie Walker, Former Sheriff Tom Farley, Supreme Court Justice Philip McCook, and Charlie Harnett, the motor vehicle commissioner.

The "Boys" have their parades, their dinners, and their socials.

"Four or five free socials each year," said Mr. Turnier. "All the old-timers come."

Mr. Turnier knew First Avenue in the days when the gas-tank district above Fifty-Ninth Street was called "Battle Row," because of the skirmishes between gangs held on this territory.

Eleven

Tea for Beekman Place

THERE is a very pretty garden at the back of One Beekman Place. It has gay little painted tables in it, cheerful bits of greenery in season, and a happy array of bright flowers. Austin Strong, the playwright, lives in the big apartment house that towers above the garden.

We walked out upon it, the morning we strolled through Beekman Place. It was as near as we got to the waterfront. Only by stepping out on this terrace could we glimpse the East River from this neighborhood.

Beekman Place crossed the half-century mark on December 15, 1933. It's a quaint section of town, safely hidden by tall buildings and separated from the main part of New York by a rather tenementy neighborhood. The people who live on the Place all know one another. They lead lives apart from the rest of the city.

The Place has had its ups and downs. As recently as in 1915, the washings of the Cohens and the Murphys flapped under the noses of their ritzy neighbors, in One Beekman Place, the first apartment-house to appear in a district given to the packing plants, breweries, and the slaughter-house gang. Except for a group of three, four-story residences, Number One shared honors with Burns Brothers Coal Yard, the old shot tower, and a huge cigar factory.

Beekman Place gets its name from the famous New York family, who originally owned the land it covers. Mrs. Steinway and I reached the Place by swinging off First Avenue to the right at Mitchell Place. The earliest records of this section of the city appear in a city Atlas of 1867. It is indicated as a proposed public street.

The pioneer apartment house of the locality holds its own in a section that probably has more head-liners to the landlord count than any other district in town.

Number One boasts for tenants, Mr. and Mrs. David Milton, son-in-law and daughter of John D. Rockefeller, Jr., Mr. and Mrs. Herbert L. Satterlee, brother-in-law and sister of J. P. Morgan, Mr. and Mrs. Lyman Beecher Stowe, Colonel William Donovan and Revell McCallum.

We liked the little houses that snuggled up against the big apartment buildings. They were very individual. Some reminded us of the picturesque Old Chelsea homes in London. Laurette

Taylor Manners lives in Number 39; James Forrestal has done all sorts of odd and interesting things to his home at Number 17.

One of the novelties of the neighborhood is William B. Leeds' penthouse at Number 30. Mr. Leeds is the skyrocketing heir to the tinplate millions.

On the same block, you will find Guthrie McClintic and his wife, Katharine Cornell; at Number 23, Captain Archie Roosevelt lives in Beekman Mansion; Mrs. A. Barton Hepburn at Number Two (she owns this apartment building) and as I have said is president of the Pan-Hellenic, which occupies Number Three Mitchell Place).

Strung on the same chain are Mitchell and Sutton Place. The former, which connects Beekman Place and First Avenue at Forty-Ninth Street, is shown on the old Atlases as an accomplished fact in 1867, although it was not officially accepted by the city until the 'nineties.

Sutton Place farther up the line was named after David V. Button's grandfather, Effingham Sutton, who owned this section at the foot of East Fifty-Seventh Street in the nineteenth century. He let the property go a few years before the booming of the neighborhood. It shot up to the million mark in value, shortly after he sold the land.

David Sutton is the president of the First Avenue Association.

There are two yacht landings on the East River, that of the New York Yacht Club at the foot of Twenty-Sixth Street, and the floating dock at the foot of East Fifty-Second Street, where the residents of River House may come ashore, or embark.

It is fashionable to have an East River address. One of the smartest places to live is River House. It is built in three units, all entered by a main hall which overlooks the water. There is a garden just outside the wall. On spring and early summer evenings, a fountain plays in the little semi-court; from it, you can see Welfare Island.

River House is cooperative. The tenants own their apartments. Among them are Mr. and Mrs. Cornelius Vanderbilt Whitney, Mr. and Mrs. Marshall Field, Mr. and Mrs. Bradford Norman, Jr., and Mr. and Mrs. William Breed.

The majority are also members of the River Club, with its squash and tennis courts, swimming pool, and ballroom. Everything is done on a very gorgeous scale. The apartments are duplexes. Much of the paneling is glass.

Those who make use of the yacht landing include Mr. and Mrs. Marshall Field and Mr. and Mrs. Harold Talbott, Jr. In the spring and summer, they commute to and from their Long Island country places in express cruisers. Vincent Astor frequently drops the *Nourmahal's* anchor off East Fifty-Second Street to send a tender ashore for William Rhinelander Stewart, who has started on many cruises from this point of departure. Douglas Fairbanks once sent eighty trunks ashore from some yacht or other to the River House landing.

Across the street from River House is the Mayfair Yacht Club, a lunching and dining place where Dwight Fiske, who pokes sardonic fun at society, sings.

Several of the most artistically decorated apartments in the city are contained in River House.

There is the Cornelius Vanderbilt Whitney townhome, for example, on the sixth floor in the left wing of River House. The library overlooks the water. It is gay, cheerful, and friendly, bright with raspberry red hangings and brilliant cushions. The walls are paneled in natural walnut.

Chalk white is the color theme of Mrs. Bradford Norman's apartment. The walls are white and the furniture is white. The great concert grand piano at the far end of the living room is ebony black and so are the negro minstrels sketched in bold strokes on the broad expanse of mirror that covers the entire south wall. The same dead white hangings and upholstery are used in the dining room at the opposite end of the apartment.

William Rhinelander Stewart, whose family history is closely linked with Washington Square, is also a tenant in River House. The decorations of his duplex apartment, including the living room on the first floor and the sitting room on the second, are done in white. The little sitting room has an old-fashioned bay window in it, that overlooks the East River. Here, Mr. Stewart has his desk. How he ever writes any letters I don't know; I am sure I should be always peeping at the big and little boats constantly moving back and forth on the river.

Just across from River House is Welfare Island. The grim gray buildings that flank the narrow strip of land which extends from East Fiftieth to East Eighty-Fifth Streets, rise like some medieval fortress above the swift black waters.

Mr. Stewart tells me that he has often gone with his father, the late William Rhinelander Stewart, Senior, to see the island. His father was President of the State Board of Charities for twenty-five years.

Old Mr. Stewart was a fine type of New Yorker. Up to the time of his death, he served as Junior Warden of Grace Church, and in the last years of his life wrote a very comprehensive book on the history of Grace Church and old New York. He lived at 701 Park Avenue, the site of the new Union Club building.

Twelve

❧❧❧

The Rise of the Walkup

GARDEN BACK OF RE-MODELLED
PHIPPS' TENEMENT
QUEENSBORO BRIDGE IN REAR

WHEN we left Beekman Place, we detoured back to First Avenue. Two old breweries and a block of Greenwich Villagey houses greeted us. Those whose incomes were knocked galley-west in the crash, with former champagne tastes and present-day beer incomes, have dubbed the gay row of merry-looking remodeled tenements that skirt the East River from Fifty-Fifth to Fifty-Sixth Streets, The Ark.

During the depression the Phipps estate, owners of the property, converted the buildings into very livable studio apartments.

They have out-arted Greenwich Village in the bizarre color schemes used; scarlet, blue, yellow, and green doors are the rule and not the exception. Equally startling are the interior decorations. Mrs. Steinway and I peeked in a lovely old-fashioned garden at the rear of these ultra-modernistic apartments. It is walled-in.

We reached it through an apartment that was being re-modeled. The entire row overlooks this beautiful garden, bright, when we looked at it in May, with quaint flowers, flagged walks, and gaily painted chairs and tables. The view of the East River was quite magnificent from this point. To the north, we saw the spectacular and massive span of the Queensborough Bridge.

Directly across were the gloomy gray buildings of Welfare, or Blackwell's Island.

As far back as our history goes, there has always been some-thing official about Blackwell's Island, the slim strip of land that runs up the middle of the East River from Fifty-First Street to Eighty-Sixth Street.

In the time of the Dutch, it was known as the Long Island, then Nassau Island, Blackwell's, and, finally, Welfare.

John Manning, captain of a trading vessel that plied between

LOOKING ACROSS BLACKWELL'S
ISLAND TO EAST RIVER SHORE

New York and New Haven, gave up his calling for a commission in the Revolutionary forces. He was appointed sheriff of New York after the first conquest by the British. From the fruits of that office, he purchased the Long Island. In 1674 Manning's political star set. On the steps of the Old Stadt Haus at Coenties Slip he was forever barred from holding public office. He retired to his East River island to enjoy the luxurious home he had built himself. Having money, he had friends too, of a kind. His house was noted for its hospitable board. His dinners were famed.

When Manning died, he bequeathed his island to his daughter who married Robert Blackwell, for whom it was renamed. The city purchased its one hundred and twenty acres in 1828 at a cost of fifty thousand dollars. Since that time, it has been used for an almshouse, prison, and hospital quarters.

At regular intervals, public-minded citizens step forward with the suggestion that the city remove the prison, almshouse, and hospital from Welfare Island and that it be turned into a public park.

Someday it may be done. The island is naturally beautiful in spite of the grim fortress-like gray stone buildings that cover it.

It was Mrs. Tuckerman Draper who convinced the Phipps estate that the dilapidated tenements which edged First Avenue between Fifty-Fifth and Fifty-Sixth Streets, could be remodeled into English flats. They say she had in mind the buildings along the Thames in London. The success of the idea was based on the rise of the walk-up during the Depression.

Among the interesting apartments leased by fashionable New Yorkers is that occupied by Mr. and Mrs. Goodhue Livingston.

Vogue thought so much of it that they ran a two-page spread of the Livingston apartment.

They say it was about 1920 that the original group of fashionable New Yorkers took possession of the Sutton Place neighborhood. The first block to be touched was on the east side of Avenue A between Fifty-Seventh and Fifty-Eighth Streets where an entire row of Georgian houses was reclaimed and the backyards transformed into gardens.

John Phipps and Mrs. Frederick Guest were among the early settlers. The former occupies an apartment in the huge thirteen-story cooperative house erected at One Sutton Place South in 1925.

They say that Sutton Place was first owned by Thomas Pearsall, a farmer. "Boss" Tweed bought some of his land; he purchased it from the Pearsall heirs.

But it was not until Effingham B. Sutton, owner of a clipper-ship line, came along in 1875 and tried to start a real-estate boom, by moving from his home at Fifth Avenue and Sixteenth Street to a house built on the site now occupied by Mrs. Vanderbilt's home, that interest centered on the locality. Mr. Sutton's business partner was James Stokes, also a prominent merchant in the Mauve Decade and father of Anson Phelps Stokes. The two formed a syndicate and acquired considerable property in the Avenue A district between Fifty-Eighth and Sixtieth Streets. The boom failed to materialize.

The first record of the section appears in the New York Directory of 1884 and on Bromley's map published two years later.

In June of 1897, the residents petitioned the Board of Aldermen to name officially Avenue A from Fifty-Seventh to Sixtieth Streets—Sutton Place.

The modern Sutton Place extends all the way from East Fifty-Third to East Sixtieth in the first block back of the waterfront. But the name was originally given to the high river-front section of Avenue A opposite Welfare Island where it formed a cul de sac at the end of East Fifty-Eighth Street and Riverview Terrace.

David Sutton, the grandson of Effingham B. Sutton, for whom Sutton Place was named, was active in the erection of the first cooperative apartment house on East Fifty-Seventh Street—a point, in view of the fact that he achieved the goal his grandfather set—the reclamation of the East River waterfront in the 'fifties and 'sixties.

Life in this section is a neighborhood matter. The people all know one another. They belong to the same crowd and go to the same parties.

In the winter they skate on Rip Dolman's tennis court at the southwest corner of Fifty-Seventh Street and Sutton Place. He floods it every night. Electric lights in all colors brighten it. Gaby Lyons, the skating instructor, has taught all of the children in the neighborhood to cut figure eights.

The Ark faces the crumbling walls of two breweries. Directly across is the former Peter Doelger Brewery. This section was once an all-brewery neighborhood. The district still bears trace of the German influence. The first influx of Germans swept in during the middle of the nineteenth century. A few settlers who remember this neighborhood live in the alley I call Sally's.

That's just the name for Riverview Terrace, the quaint little street which is a block long and extends only from Fifty-Eighth to Fifty-Ninth Street above the waterfront, back of Sutton Place. Ancient cobblestones pave it. Heavily leafed maples shadow it and spring flowers give it color.

A single row of brownstone-front houses lines the west side of River Terrace. They face the river. Private families occupy them. The sort of people who pride themselves in living in their own homes. Windows and gardens were gay with iris and hyacinths the May afternoon Mrs. Steinway and I explored the street.

Great purple iris filled the brass bowl that brightened the front window of Miss Anna Curtis's house at Number Four.

"But I'm not really a first family here," she protested laughingly. "To be sure, I've lived in the neighborhood all my life, but I have been at Number Four only ten years!"

The Miltons used to live in Miss Curtis's house. Mrs. Paula Milton came back to see it a few days before we visited the place, and to reminisce.

"She was here the year of the great blizzard," said Miss Curtis. "One of her neighbors who lived at Number Five fell in a drift in front of this house. He was rescued through the parlor windows. The snow had drifted so high they could not get the front door open."

In more recent years society has made a stronghold of Sutton Place. The older residents are proud of their new neighbors. "Dr. Foster Kennedy lives across the street," said Miss Curtis, nodding in the direction of Fifty-Eighth Street. "And so does Mrs. W. K. Vanderbilt, and all those folks. But I don't think they love their homes as much as we do."

There are other links with the past not far from Sally's Alley.

An ancient milestone and a small farmhouse are within the

reach of fashionable Sutton Place. The milestone was a guide to the weary traveler coming to the city. It still stands right where it was placed, on what is now the northwest corner of Fifty-Seventh Street and Third Avenue. It bears the inscription "4 Miles to City Hall."

One block down, on the southeast corner of Fifty-Sixth Street and Third Avenue, a tiny brown wooden house nestles between tall buildings. It is known as "the Old Norwood Place" and is owned by Jerry O'Leary, political boss of the district.

Within shouting distance of the Norwood homestead, is the most luxurious residential section of New York City.

Anne Morgan and Mrs. W. K. Vanderbilt put it on the map. Miss Morgan lives at Number Three Sutton Place, while Mrs. Vanderbilt is her next-door neighbor at Number One. Across the way at Number One Sutton Place, South, Mrs. Charles Sabin makes her home in a spacious apartment overlooking the East River.

On top of 444 East Fifty-Seventh Street, we find the duplex apartment of the Jay Goulds, the latter a grandson of the famous Jay Gould who had a spectacular Wall Street career.

A few floors below the Goulds dwell Mr. and Mrs. Jerome Napoleon Bonaparte in an Empire green-hued apartment that faces the East River. For several years many of the treasures of the Patterson as well as a few of the Bonaparte family were housed within these four walls, including a tea set that boasts Napoleon's crest. These museum pieces are now in storage.

The interest for us, however, in this section, lay on the waterfront. We glimpsed it not only at Riverview Terrace but also at Sutton Place, where we could walk to the end of Fifty-Seventh

Street and look out over the shrubbery of the adjoining gardens, down upon Blackwell's or Welfare Island.

The vast span of the Queensborough Bridge cast its shadow over us, as we turned back from Sutton Place and Riverview Terrace to First Avenue. Power plants again barred us from the waterfront. Those beneath the bridge belong to the New York Steam Corporation. Stored power of another sort flanked First Avenue, in the great gas tanks that serve as landmarks along waterfront streets. In recent years their dull brown sides have been repainted a multi-toned blue, green, and red camouflaged pattern.

After one short block of the street that becomes York Avenue after it crossed Fifty-Ninth Street, we turned off again toward East River.

Thirteen

Automobile Avenue

A RIVERFRONT DINER.

THIS is another Marginal Street. It breaks out several times on the East as well as the West Side. For some reason or other, it seems to have made a hit with motorists and automobile salesmen. The street is wide and little traveled. They can speed up and down it to their heart's content.

Mrs. Steinway says that on Sunday mornings it is crammed with parked cars being repaired. Their owners bring them to Marginal Street to tinker on tires, and engines. Their families come too; the children play along the docks while the father works on the flivver.

That great big white skyscraper at Sixty-Sixth and Marginal

Street is the Rockefeller Hospital. It is built on the site of an old white-pillared mansion erected shortly after the Revolution.

The ground once belonged to the Schermerhorn family. Up to the time the Rockefellers purchased the property, the Schermerhorn mansion was intact. Close by it stood the chapel where the family worshiped.

Long after the Schermerhorns had gone to glory, the Pastime Athletic Club took possession of the estate. The chapel became the clubhouse. It was a white frame building with slanting roof and Colonial pillars. Sloping from the house and chapel to the river was a stretch of green lawn, bordered by meadows. At the entrance to the grounds were a number of graves, three on either side of the path that led to the mansion. Close by the old headstones towered a majestic oak tree, and near the tree was a hollow spot in the ground. This marked the burial vault of the Schermerhorns.

The mansion, Felix Oldboy says, was an ambitious structure of two stories and a half, topped off by a cupola or Captain's walk. It commanded a view of Hell Gate and the East River Islands. The Schermerhorns at one time owned much real estate in the neighborhood and several houses built by various branches of the extensive family. Their neighbors were the Joneses for whom Jones' Wood, which stood beyond the Schermerhorn House, was named, the Winthrops, Dunscombs, Kings, and Hoffmans.

The little colony was mainly Episcopalians. Often because of yellow fever scourges in the city, these families remained late in the season at their country places. Feeling the need for a church, they applied to the vestry of Trinity for assistance. The result was St. James Church, erected on the corner of Sixty-Ninth

Street and Lexington Avenue and consecrated by Bishop Moore. It was a plain wooden structure with a tiny steeple; a country church surrounded by farms. Peter Schermerhorn was a St. James warden.

The spire of St. James now rises at Madison Avenue and Seventy-First Street and is one of the city's most fashionable churches. The great white cubicles of the Rockefeller Institute tower above Schermerhorn Heights.

It was long past one o'clock and drizzling a little when we turned up Marginal Street. So great had been our interest in the walk that we had forgotten the time. We were hungry. We stood for a few minutes at the corner above the Rockefeller Institute deciding where to eat.

Coal barges flanked the waterfront. Near a truck, we caught sight of a little diner shining with new paint and sporting a jaunty red and white striped awning. Above it, loomed up the sign "Joe's Hot Dog Stand, Ladies Welcome."

"Let's try it," said Mrs. Steinway.

It was very pleasant. We sat out on a little side porch, facing the water. Between barges, we caught glimpses of river traffic. Our hamburger steak sandwiches were fresh and hot and the beer foaming. The cost was twenty cents apiece.

Joe and his wife did the cooking. "We hope to get a good crowd here this summer," they said. "But it isn't half bad now. The interns and nurses come down from the hospital. They keep us busy."

At Seventy-First Street we were again forced away from the waterfront, back onto the former First Avenue, now York Avenue. The name has changed the character. Old tenements are slicked up. Fresh fronts have been put on stores and a better class of tenants bid for them. Though still in the transitory stage, York Avenue is far better than First Avenue ever thought of being.

"I went to that school when it was down on Forty-Fourth Street," Mrs. Steinway said, as we passed a very modern-looking Colonial brick building on East Eighty-Third Street, near the river. It was the Brearley School that numbered among its recent pupils, Doris Duke, America's tobacco heiress.

The Brearley School was founded in 1883 by Mr. Samuel Brearley, A. B., Harvard, 1871, winner of the first Bowdoin Prize, and first Headmaster of the School. He died in 1886 and was succeeded by Mr. James G. Crosswell, A. B., Harvard, 1873, who was Headmaster for twenty-eight years.

In 1889 the School was incorporated as The Brearley School, Ltd., the incorporators being the Reverend William R. Huntington, Mrs. F. A. Paddock, Mrs. Joseph H. Choate, Mrs. James J. Higginson, Messrs. George C. Clark, Charles C. Beaman and Albert Stickney. A schoolhouse was erected at Number 17 West Forty-Fourth Street.

In 1912 the outstanding stock of the corporation was transferred to Henry Fairfield Osborne, George C. Clark, Cleveland H. Dodge, Pierre Jay, and Lewis Cass Ledyard, as trustees. In the same year, a new schoolhouse was built at Park Avenue and Sixty-First Street and occupied in the autumn. It was sold in 1929. The present building, on the bank of the East River and Eighty-Third Street, is the home of one of the important private schools of New York City.

Fourteen

A Friend of John Jacob Astor

THE Doctors' Hospital, that huge white stone building at the southwest corner of Eighty-Eighth Street and East End Avenue, is on the site of the original John Jacob Astor country home.

Spring flowers were blooming in the little Carl Schurz Park opposite the hospital, the morning we came by. The old white frame house placed Cater-cornered in the park is the Gracie Mansion, now owned by the Museum of the City of New York. As I write this chapter, plans are being drawn for a beer garden to be built in Carl Schurz Square.

Archibald Gracie was a neighbor of John Jacob Astor, and a friend of Washington Irving, frequent guest at the Astor country home. In his journal of January 1813, Irving writes," Mr. Gracie has moved into his new house and I find a very warm reception at the fireside."

Gracie was a famous New York merchant. He and his neighbors, the Rhinelanders, and Mr. Astor brought fame and prosperity to Yorkville. If you visit his house today, you will see that there is quite a bit of ground between it and the river. At the time it was built, the shore practically touched the side foundations. Much earth has evidently been filled in since.

It was said of Mr. Gracie's home when it was built, "The mansion is elegant in the modern style, and the grounds are laid out with a taste in gardens."

The house faces a bend in the river known as Horn's Hook, also called Gracie Point and Rhinelander Neck.

Until 1932, the Gracie Mansion housed the Museum of the City of New York, which has since moved to its new quarters at One Hundred and Fourth Street and Fifth Avenue. However, the Gracie home is still used as an overflow museum. It is well worth visiting.

Before tall buildings loomed up on the waterfront, the Gracie mansion was a landmark to those who navigated the dangerous waters of Hell Gate. Now the Doctors' Hospital guides the river-craft. At night a huge sign illuminates its roof, not only as a signpost for mariners, but also to warn them not to blow their boat whistles in front of the hospital, if they can help it.

Mr. Astor himself passed the hot weather months in the house that overlooked Hell Gate. If his summer home were standing today, it would be in the heart of New York City. Then it was far out in the country.

Washington Irving, in a letter to his brother, Peter Irving, writes, "I have been quartered for a month at Hell Gate with Mr. Astor, and I have not had so quiet or delightful time since I have been in America. He has a spacious and well-built house, with a lawn in the front of it and a garden in the rear. The lawn sweeps down to the water's edge, and full in front of the house is the little strait of Hell Gate, which forms a constantly moving picture."

By a curious trick of fate, the great-great-grandson of John Jacob Astor returned to the spot where a century before the Astor home had been. On the twenty-seventh of November, 1933, young John Jacob Astor's mother, Mrs. Madeleine Force Astor Dick, was married in the Doctors' Hospital to Enzo Fiermonte, an Italian. Mr. Astor was present at the wedding.

Fabulous stories have been told of the Doctors' Hospital. They have gained in the telling. In reality, it is nothing more nor less than a well-equipped apartment hotel run as a medical unit. The most expensive floor is the tenth. Here the rooms are thirty-five dollars a day. The average room is ten dollars a day. At that, however, it is the only hospital of its kind in New York. The Board of Directors includes two members of the firm of J. P. Morgan and Company. The head physician is Dr. Alexander Lambert, one of the most celebrated surgeons in the country.

Mrs. Steinway and I climbed to the roof of the hospital to get a view of the East River. The fourteenth floor is used as a solarium. From it, convalescing patients may watch, as old Mr. Astor and Mr. Gracie once did from their front porches, the churning waters of the most dangerous point in the East River.

Hell Gate has come down through history as a devil's pool.

It lies directly opposite the Doctors' Hospital and the Gracie Mansion. The shore that you see beyond is that of Astoria.

The morning that we watched the narrow straits of Hell Gate, the water was as peaceful and placid as one might wish. This was because of low tide. As the tide turns, the stream begins to fret, at half-tide it boils into seething whirlpools. When the tide is full, it swishes back into a gentle river.

They say that out of sheer spleen because so many of their people had come to grief in it, the Dutch christened the channel Hell-Gat, and the English translated it into Hell Gate. For many years a series of little rocks could be seen rising in the center of the channel; they were called the Hen and Chickens. In early American records, I find tales of a pirate ship wrecked on these rocks. The vessel lay there for many years. Another legend concerns a murder committed on the Hen and Chickens. Jutting out into Hell Gate is the tip-end of Blackwell's or Welfare Island. At the opposite end of Hell Gate, to the north of the Gracie Mansion, rises a small island known as Mill Rock, and just beyond it are Ward's and Randall's Islands. There is nothing much to Mill Rock now. In years gone by it used to be called Sandy Gibson's Island, because Sandy lived on it and served clam chowder to those who rowed over to pay him a visit. Striped bass fishing was good from his rocks.

Former Park Commissioner Walter Herrick lives in one of those old-fashioned red-brick houses that flank the Doctors' Hospital. His number is 148. Mr. Herrick is a pioneer in this neighborhood. He knew it in the days when nothing but German was spoken in Carl Schurz Park.

An angle in the river, where it forks out to branch into Long

Island Sound, changes it into the Harlem River. Ward's Island is the dividing line. This may be plainly seen from the roof of any tall building on East End Avenue, or from the docks at the foot of Ninety-First Street. Near Ninety-First Street and East End Avenue is Poverty Row, the nice old-fashioned apartment houses made smart by Vincent Astor.

Once off York into East End Avenue, we entered a different neighborhood. From Eighty-Sixth Street to Ninety-First, the blocks are suggestive of Pomander Walk. Trees, the little Park, and rows of old-timey houses make this section a charming residential locality. Beyond lies the fringe of Harlem's Little Italy, the second-largest Italian city in the world.

The border-line is the new playground which occupies the former site of the old House of Mercy, a Catholic home for wayward girls.

Henry Nerge, secretary of the Yorkville Chamber of Commerce, gives the dividing lines of Yorkville as Fifty-Ninth Street and One Hundred and Tenth, from Fifth Avenue to the East River.

The homey smell of hops heralds the industry of the neighborhood. The fragrance was carried to us by a land breeze that May afternoon.

In the brewery group, the most spectacular figure is Colonel Jacob Ruppert, owner of The Yankees. True to tradition, the Ruppert family lived near the brewery at 1639 Third Avenue, which brought them fame. Its great brick smokestacks may be seen from the waterfront.

The Ehret breweries have been closed since 1917 when the Volstead Act was signed. Even with the Repeal of the Eighteenth

Amendment, no signs of opening up the big cream brick breweries have been evidenced. They lie on East Ninetieth Street, not far from the river.

Breweries, beer gardens, and Yorkville are synonymous. One of the most famous gardens used to stand near the water's edge at the foot of East Ninety-First Street. Melodeon Hall was the name of it. The ornate building now shelters a quick lunch emporium. There are several vacant lots along the waterfront in this vicinity that would lend themselves to a grand beer garden site. So far, no one has taken advantage of the idea. The present beer gardens of Yorkville have an emphasis on the beer and not the garden.

The ferry to Astoria leaves from the foot of East Ninety-First Street. It leads to the little town where the Steinway pianos are made. For many years the old Steinway mansion was the showplace of that neighborhood. Though the Steinways have long since moved to New York, their factories are still in Astoria and the Long Island settlement is famous because of the Steinway name.

Fifteen

The Farmer's Market

WEST WASHINGTON MARKET
TRUCK

RUSSELL SCHALLER is president of the Harlem Market. His memories of New York date back to 1891, when the market opened. He is a big, red-cheeked, hearty-voiced man, with a kindly face and a great sense of humor. He gave Theodore Steinway his first job. It was checking up on billboard posters of North Beach, an amusement park in which the Ehrets and Mr. Schaller were interested.

We all met for luncheon one noon to discuss our walk—Mrs. Steinway and myself, Mr. Schaller, and Mr. Steinway.

"Russell paid me three dollars a week," Mr. Steinway said.

"And raised you fifty cents at the end of two weeks," spoke up Mr. Schaller. "I did that because I gave you lists of billboard locations that never existed. When you came back and said they were not there I knew you had at least been working."

The Harlem Market is the one privately owned market in New York. It runs from One Hundred and Second to One Hundred and Third Street across from the East River to First Avenue. Only farmers who raise their own produce are permitted to rent space in it.

Most of them have been coming to it ever since the market opened. There is John Luck, for example—seventy-four years old and still going strong. He's a big, husky, red-faced fellow, with a handle-bar mustache and a huge body, toughened by years of hard work. Charles Bittall, the farmer who likes the ponies as well as truck gardening, is another old-timer.

Two people instrumental in building up the Market were the late William Steinway and the late George Ehret. These gentlemen owned North Beach, a summer resort, William Steinway for the furtherance of his trolley road from Ninety-Second Street Ferry and Thirty-Fourth Street Ferry, and George Ehret for the sale of his beer.

They first purchased the New York and College Point Ferry plying between East Ninety-Ninth Street and College Point. To stimulate business on the ferry they incorporated the Harlem Market.

In the early nineties and up to as late as 1900 and 1901, the Long Island farmers brought their produce in horse-drawn conveyances, and to save the long haul from College Point through Astoria and Corona they patronized the ferry.

In the first years of the Market, the Company was

unsuccessful, and the two incorporators aided the Company materially financially.

Louis von Bernuth, son-in-law of William Steinway, having married Paula Steinway, Theodore Steinway's half-sister, was elected president of the Harlem Market.

Russell Schaller was his secretary. Upon the death of Louis von Bernuth in 1907, Mr. Schaller came in close contact with all the farmers. In 1920, Mr. Schaller assumed control of the Market. It has prospered up to this day.

Farmers were induced to come from all parts of the country. In the last few years, they have traveled from Maine, New Hampshire, Massachusetts, New Jersey, Delaware, Maryland, and as far up New York State as Syracuse.

Now, the automobile trucks carry as much as three or four of the old horse-drawn vehicles brought to the Market.

The creation of the Harlem Market developed all the property on both sides of First Avenue from Ninety-Ninth Street to One Hundred and Sixth Street.

At one time the East River encroached upon the Market at least two hundred feet from the waterfront. Later the city built a sea wall, and Marginal Street, or Exterior Street, as they call it, which they intend to extend along the entire East River to the South Ferry, was constructed, similar to West Street on the west side of New York City.

For many years Theodore Steinway was treasurer of the Company.

I visited the Market twice. The first time with Mrs. Steinway on the third installment of our walk. It had been a day of sunlight and showers. We had started from Bellevue, in the rain, about ten o'clock in the morning. By afternoon, the skies were clearing.

We reached the Harlem Market at about three in the afternoon.

It was one of the most picturesque sections we had crossed. Even more quaint, perhaps, than the old shipyard district on South Street, because that suggested the past, while this dealt with the present.

Great wooden sheds extended out over the sidewalks. The smell of celery, spring onions, young cabbage, and ripening fruit was in the air. Since the Harlem Market does not deal in meat, that butcher-shop aroma of packing-house districts was missing.

Three o'clock in the afternoon is the end of the day for market people. The stalls, shops, and restaurants were deserted.

"Night's the time to see this place," an old market hand said. "Everybody's sleeping now."

"Where do they sleep?" I asked.

"In them hotels," he answered, pointing to two-story brick buildings plastered with such signs as "Farmer's Hotel," or "The Harlem Market Rest."

"Where do they eat?"

"In Drumm's." He nodded at a substantial-looking restaurant to our left. "That's been here ever since the Market opened."

We walked down toward the river. Ahead of us, loomed the green banks of Ward's Island. The little street—like a private lane—was paved with cobblestones. Hitching posts lined the sides. Horses and wagons had evidently once been plentiful. We found charm and individuality in the tiny, one-and-two-story buildings that encircled the court. It was another world.

I saw it again, a month later, under different circumstances. It was on a hot night in July after the Baer-Schmelling fight at the Yankee Stadium, a night too hot for New York to sleep. The streets surrounding the Market were crowded with men, women, and children, unable to stay in the sunbaked tenements.

Mr. Schaller brought a party of us to the Market. "Four o'clock in the morning is the time to see it," he said. We stayed until six, watching the great trucks, armies of men, and boy-drawn carts, mill around the square. Flaming red torches lighted the scene as dawn came.

Our front-row seats were in the small building at the west end of the Market square where the business of the Harlem Market has been carried on since the day, or night, it opened. It was an old-timey office, with a coal stove in the center, a heavy walnut desk near the window, and a well-worn directors' table for furnishing, together with several cane chairs and an almanac.

The day Mrs. Steinway and I rummaged through the Market, the office was closed.

Ward's Island which faces the Farmer's Market, like Blackwell's, is covered with city institutions but retains much of its early beauty. You can see the island very clearly from the docks that fringe the East Nineties and the Harlem Market.

Woulter Van Twiller found fine pasturage on it for his cattle in the early sixteen hundreds. The British found fine camping sites for their soldiers during the Revolutionary War. In maps of that time, it was known as Buchanan's Island. The man who drew one map marked a house at the northeast corner. This must have been about the period that five thousand Hessian and English troops were camped on the island.

On the southwest corner was the little burying ground where, in years gone by, the mounds were distinctly marked by a boulder at the head of each. The local people spoke of them as Indian mounds, but it is generally supposed that they were the graves of British soldiers.

After the Revolution, the island was divided up into farmland. In 1812 a cotton mill of solid stone, three stories high, was run up on the site now occupied by the institutional administration buildings. A wooden bridge broad enough to take a horse and wagon was built over the East River at One Hundred and Fourteenth Street and over the northwest end of the island on stone piles.

A land boom was expected to follow, but it didn't. The War of 1812 cut it short. The mill could not be run because cotton couldn't be sent up from the South. The scheme failed. In the 1840s, the Emigration Commission took possession of Ward's Island. Since then the city has made use of the property. The insane asylum now covers a good portion of it.

Randall's Island used to be a favorite feeding ground of wild birds. Bluebirds, catbirds, bobolinks, and thrushes nested here each spring in syringas and lilac bushes.

Nineteenth-century New Yorkers made the little island a picnic ground. It grew to be the fashion to row across from Manhattan Island with the family for Saturday picnics. Fishing for striped bass from Randall's Island shores was a favorite pastime.

At the time of the Revolution, Randall's Island bore the name of Montressor. Originally it was Little Barent's Island. This was corrupted into Little Barn Island. In 1732 Elias Pipon bought it and built his home on it. He named it Belle Island. Fifteen years later George Talbot purchased it, settled on it, and gave Belle his own name. In 1772 he sold the island to Captain John Montressor, who was living on it when the British took possession. In the spring of 1784 Montressor's Island was purchased by Samuel Ogden, who sold it in the fall of that same year to Jonathan Randal for twenty-four pounds. The city bought Randal's Island from the executors of this gentleman's estate in 1835 for fifty thousand dollars. It was the city that added the extra I to Randal's name.

The most thrilling period in the history of the little island was the night of September twenty-fourth in the year 1776 when a battalion of picked Continental soldiers, under the direction of Major Henly, descended upon Montressor's Island, then occupied by the British. A shot prematurely fired threw a monkey-wrench into the expedition. Twenty-two men were lost by the Americans, among them Major Henly. This was the one and only battle ever fought on any of the smaller East River Islands.

Sixteen

❧

The Rag Market

THE RAG-MAN.

LIKE some huge flower-bed, sprawled across city pavements, off One Hundred and Fifteenth Street and the East River, stretch New York's Rag Market.

All day long, hand-propelled pushcarts and horse-drawn wagons rattle over the asphalt, bringing rags to market. They are gathered by Jewish and Italian peddlers from old attics wholesale houses and ash-bins. Anything and everything in the way of cloth is grist for their mill.

Great scales manipulated by women, weigh out the bundles of rags. It was sometimes difficult for us to distinguish the women from the rags. They were large, bulging old peasants that might have been so many sacks tied in the middle.

While rag yards dot the waterfront, the only point at which they, assume the proportions of a market is on East One Hundred and Fifteenth Street. Here, one stable after another is given over to the business of juggling rag bundles. They bring three cents a pound. Paper mills buy them from the peddlers.

The Harlem Rag Market has been in existence since the middle nineteenth century. City Hall statistics show that there are some five thousand "I Cash Clothes" and rag men doing business on New York streets.

Down through the years, they have clung to the chimes of their trade, cow-bells strung on a rope suspended from two poles attached to their carts and wagons. The metallic clank of the old bells brings a rural touch to Manhattan's busy streets.

THE RAG MARKET

Our way from the Rag Market led along First Avenue up to One Hundred and Sixteenth Street, before we could again reach the river. Push carts, sheltered by red and yellow tarpaulins, replaced the Farmer's Market and the rag exchange in rapid succession.

We missed the bright yellows, reds, and blues so dear to this Italian neighborhood when we left First Avenue for Thomas Jefferson Park, a park known to every child in the neighborhood. It is their farm, here they raise in neat rows under the supervision of the city, radishes, onions, lettuce, turnips—anything you ask for in vegetables as well as their favorite flowers.

One little Italian boy led us down to show us his radish patch, another pointed out his lettuce bed. The park borders the river. It is an oasis in a district known as the "Uptown Little Italy."

Pleasant Avenue was our next path. We were now one block from the river's edge, walking along a wide, unruffled thoroughfare, once a street given over to Harlem's first families.

Two or three times we slipped down side streets to the river's edge. But the street ends were blind, and there was no way of actually following the water, so we had to return to Pleasant Avenue.

The character of the waterfront, we found, changes at One Hundredth Street and the river. Italians are responsible. In that district which extends from One Hundred and First Street and the East River to One Hundred and Twenty-Fourth Street there are said to be more Italians to the square inch than in any other portion of New York City.

Harlem is a strange mixture of all nationalities, but from what we saw the Italians predominated. They live in a neighborhood of old Harlem houses that were once American homes. Today they bear no semblance of such a past. The Italians have seen to that. So successful have been their attempts at ornamentation that hanging vines, bits of statuary, and plaster cornices that drape the buildings suggest an Italian village rather than a cross-section of an American metropolis.

At 415 Pleasant Avenue, is a stiff, quaint little old frame farm-house with blinds half drawn in a manner that implies bitter resentment against the influx of Little Italy. The house belongs to Mrs. Hodges. She is an American, keeps lodgers, and traces her ancestry back to Colonial days.

Mrs. Hodges's house maintained a determined silence in the babel that rose about it, on our June-day walk. Shouts of children at play in the streets, the clack-clack of feminine Italian tongues from fire-escape to fire-escape, and the lilting notes of hurdy-gurdy and street carousels, made no impression upon Mrs. Hodges and her lodgers. A world undisturbed by the seething excitement that sometimes boils over in its vicinity. Strange stories have swept past Mrs. Hodges's house. There was the famous murder stable, for instance, in which thirty-four Italians met their death in a feud that even the police refused to interrupt.

We reached the beginning of the Harlem River early in June. The next spurt was our fourth in the installment trips about Manhattan Island waterfront.

Seventeen

The Old Swimming Hole

FREIGHT YARDS OFF DEATH AVE

ON OUR fourth expedition around the New York water-front, we did not make time. With an afternoon to do it in, we covered but nine blocks. There was too much to see.

That section of the Island of Manhattan which lies between One Hundred and Twenty-Sixth Street and First Avenue and One Hundred and Thirty-Fifth Street and Park Avenue, turned out to be a series of sharply defined localities.

They range from simple rural districts, concerned with bucolic pleasures, to regions that rivaled the East End of London for criminal types and squalid surroundings.

At One Hundred and Twenty-Sixth Street and First Avenue, where the first bridge crossed the Harlem River, we left the main thoroughfare to follow the waterfront again. The narrow street we chose led past a series of coal yards to a stretch of green meadow, flanked on the right by the Harlem River.

It is a region that boasts fine old mansions and first families. The green meadow just beyond the coal yards at One Hundred and Twenty-Sixth Street was once included in a portion of a Colonial estate that stretched up and over Harlem Heights.

Today it is shared by neighborhood boys and a type of old New Yorker familiar to real-estate holders of the past—the squatter.

The boys have discovered a swimming hole in the back-water of the Harlem River; the squatters, a peaceful spot in which to live without facing a rent collector.

The banks of the Harlem River, where the boys now go swimming, have had their share of romance. Here the British frigate *Hussar* sank with chests of gold aboard, carrying, it was said, shackled and helpless American prisoners. Divers have worked in vain over the spot where the English boat is supposed to have sunk. They say it is embedded in mud.

In later years the youth of this neighborhood who lived in what was then the village of Harlem fished not for gold but for flounders off these same banks. There was a remarkable old hotel at the water's edge where boats could be hired for fishing. The land belonged to the Morris family. The Colonial homestead of Gouverneur Morris stood near the mouth of the Harlem River. And not far from it was the rural residence of Lewis Morris.

Frederick Van Wyck, in his Recollections of an Old New Yorker, says that "squatter sovereignty" reigned when he was a boy from Fiftieth Street away into Central Park, then only partly developed.

"It was a picturesque settlement," he writes, "built of all the old lumber, boxes, barrels, and abandoned tin that could be found. The junk dealers who drove through the streets lived there. These junk men nagged weary, bony horses attached to many bedraggled wagons, with a string of cowbells of different sizes attached to a strap across the wagon."

"Squatterville" now trims the banks of the Harlem River. I am sure that descendants of the same tribe that Mr. Van Wyck knew as a boy must now be making homes in lean-tos up and down the river's edge. Theirs is not a B. E. F. settlement. The tiny shacks have been in place for many years. The arrangement of the furniture, the quirk of the clotheslines and the Joseph's-coat patterns on roofs reveal the familiarity of long use.

Just beyond the green meadow shared by boys and squatters is New York's chief kindling yard, and one of its oldest. It is a big place neatly stacked with all sorts of logs and kindling wood. Clark and Wilkins run it. The firm is proud of the fact that it deals only in food for fuel purposes, that it continues to deliver in horse-drawn trucks, and that it has been in business on the same spot since 1859.

The bridge that crosses the Harlem River at One Hundred and Twenty-Fifth Street and First Avenue marks the site of Johannes Verveleelyn's first ferry-house. Early records show that he was a brewery man and that he "regaled the company with generous portions of his New Amsterdam ale," during the reign of Peter Stuyvesant.

When the village of Nieuw Haarlem was founded, Verveleelyn combined the duties of innkeeper and brewer with those of ferryman. He prevailed upon Stuyvesant to select him for the ferryman of the Harlem River. His plea was granted. The start of the ferry brought fresh hope to the pioneering villagers. Verveleelyn's little inn built alongside the Indian trail brought cheer to their souls.

An exciting account of Mr. Verveleelyn's thrilling adventures as a ferryman may be read in Riker's History of Harlem.

The Dutch ferryman also piloted the boat that plied across Spuyten Duyvil. One penny silver was the cost of transporting any person. Here, too, he built an inn to take care of his passengers if they wanted to stay the night.

We lingered on the green banks of the river, just above the Harlem Bridge at One Hundred and Twenty-Fifth Street. We had crossed coal yards to reach the meadow. It was warm. To stop was pleasant, especially with a fresh little wind fanning our thin summer dresses. We wanted to sit for a while, as the people of the neighborhood were doing, on the ground, and watch the children swimming. Some of the women waded in with the kids. The family dogs joined them. Harlem was enjoying the June afternoon.

We could understand why Johannes Verveleelyn, the ferryman, had preferred it to Nieuw Amsterdam. It was away from the hustle and bustle of a town that even then must have been disturbing in its energy.

It was half past five in the afternoon when we called it a day at One Hundred and Twenty-Sixth Street and the Harlem River.

The boundary lines of the old villages that once went to make up Manhattan Island are still apparent. An abrupt change in the character of the neighborhood marks the unseen division of the little settlements that have now merged into a city of seven million.

Of all the east waterfront districts through which we passed, however, Harlem was the least changed. From the moment we left One Hundred and Twenty-Fifth Street, to follow the green banks of the winding Harlem River, we were in another town.

One Hundred and Twenty-Fifth Street marks the heart of the Nieuw Haarlem Village where, in 1658, the first settlers broke ground near the Harlem River, probably on the very spot now occupied by the squatters we met when we skirted the old swimming hole.

The pioneer of Harlem was Johannes de la Montagne, a Huguenot. He and his wife and little daughter landed at the Battery from Leyden in August of the year 1638. After resting a few days in Nieuw Amsterdam, Montagne bought a dugout canoe, put his family in it, and paddled up the East River to what is now Harlem; there he built himself a log cabin snug enough for approaching winter. Deer were plentiful on Ward's Island. There was Indian corn to eat and plenty of fish for variety.

Huge gas tanks mark the site of Montagne's home today. I believe, however, that the little neck of land which juts out into the river still bears the name of Montagne's Point.

For many years a tiny creek that had its head at One Hundred and Eleventh Street and Fifth Avenue also bore the young Huguenot's name. It is obliterated now, by apartment buildings and brownstone-front houses. At One Hundred and Ninth Street, where it emptied into the Harlem River, the creek was marked by a mill—the first in Harlem.

Church Lane, the first road through Harlem, also terminated

at the river's edge, near One Hundred and Twenty-Fifth Street. We swung along a portion of it when we left One Hundred and Twenty-Fifth Street and First Avenue to cut down by the waterfront.

Church Lane began where an Indian Trail left off at One Hundred and Seventeenth Street and Lexington Avenue.

Another historic spot touched by us, in our Harlem waterfront stroll, was the Village Green which lay at what is now the foot of One Hundred and Twenty-Fourth Street and Pleasant Avenue. The street is a dead end.

The crumbling shacks, rotting boats, and general down-at-the-heels air tell nothing of the past beauty of the location where in the seventeenth century, stalwart Dutch burghers paddled up in their solid dugouts from New York—an eight-mile journey.

Though the rickety buildings that line the river sport the names of boat clubs, I doubt if very few of the men who belong do any active sailing on the Harlem.

As for the houses at One Hundred and Twenty-Fourth Street —the majority are occupied by Italians. They say they are Sicilians. The pink and blue stucco which they have plastered on the old brownstone fronts, gives strength to this belief. There is a touch of Naples in the color scheme.

In 1666, Richard Nicolls, the first English Governor of New York, set the boundary lines of Harlem Village from One Hundred and Seventeenth Street and Lexington to One Hundred and Seventh Street and Seventh Avenue, from there across to the point about where Grant's Tomb now stands, then north to Spuyten Duyvil Creek and on over to the East River down as far as Seventy-Fourth Street.

Not far from the lumberyard where we stopped to talk with the old man about firewood lay the first church burying ground of Nieuw Haarlem, just below what is now Itch Park. The land back of the present lumberyard was used in Dutch Harlem days for gardens. Carrying out a custom of Holland, the settlers had their homes on one piece of ground and their gardens on another.

Montagne the younger lived in a cozy little wooden house at First Avenue and Church Lane, which would now be about One Hundred and Twenty-Fifth Street and First Avenue. The burying ground lay to the north of him and the gardens to the west.

Doctor Montagne, his father, died in 1670 and was put to rest in the tiny burying ground which the lumberyard now covers.

The Third Avenue Bridge, which crosses the Harlem River above the lumberyard and this side of Itch Park, is built on the foundations of the first wooden structure to be spanned across the Harlem River.

Today there are nine bridges across the Harlem.

Eighteen

Scratch Park

GRANT'S TOMB
AND RIVERSIDE CHURCH
FROM THE WATERFRONT

THE shadows were lengthening when we left the lumberyard. It was late afternoon.

"If ye go any further," said the lumberyard proprietor, "I'd carry a stick or something along with ye. There's tough characters beyond." He shook his head as we started off.

"We're not afraid," we answered. But we were. Great, funnel-like coal chutes ran a network of lines overhead. Our road dipped away from the river into a tunnel formed by the Third Avenue L tracks and car barns. It was dark. The street lights had not been turned on. Dimly we could distinguish slouching figures leaning against the sides of buildings. One man lay on the sidewalk; we almost tripped over him. Another, stretched out in the gutter, was asleep or drunk.

There was an ominous air of silence about the tunnel-like street. Far away we could hear the roar of an approaching train. We hurried on. The sinister quality of the neighborhood suggested only one other section of town we had found along the waterfront: that district beneath the Manhattan Bridge. It was more ominous.

Suddenly the street curved. We were again in the daylight.

"I'm glad we're out of that!" Ruth Steinway exclaimed.

We were once more on the waterfront. Our tunnel had brought us to One Hundred and Thirtieth Street and Third Avenue, the point where the Avenue crosses the Harlem River.

Low, old-fashioned, red-brick buildings stretched to the left. Ahead was a pretty green triangular strip of grass and trees.

"What a nice park," I said.

It was at first sight. But on the benches, on the grass, and sprawled across the walks lay ragged, dirty, unkempt-looking men and women!

"Sure," said Policeman Gavigan, of the Twenty-Fifth Police Precinct, "ye're in the center of Scratch or Itch Park."

The cheap rooming houses and dives that extend from Park Avenue and One Hundred and Twenty-Ninth Street across to Third, pour their backwash into Scratch Park.

The police give it the once-over whenever they are looking for criminals.

"Has it any other names?" I asked Gavigan.

"Plenty, but they're not printable."

"Has the park any history?"

"I'll say it has. Been there long enough."

Some of the stories are to do with the women. Drab, dreary yarns. There is that one about Mary Brown.

"She never fails to visit us," John Hartmayer, also of the neighborhood police station, remarked. " Mary's an old friend and a resident of Scratch Park, when she isn't with us."

"What's her story?"

"Oh, it's not a big one. She had a little money. Somebody got it. She took to drink. She's going on forty-eight or fifty now—we've known her about fifteen years."

Mary is only one of the many women in Scratch Park.

"The Place Where the Derelict Follies Girls Go, is another name you might give the park," suggested Patrolman Gavigan.

The women resented us. They stared with hostile eyes as we hurried through the little park. A strange crowd they were—with their wispy hair, seared faces, and dirty clothing.

Some date back to Bowery days.

"But as far as that goes," said John Hartmayer, "this is really a continuation of the Bowery."

When the lower end of the famous street was cleaned out, the people moved north.

"They call this section the 'Uptown Bowery,'" said Gavigan.

It looked the part. Cheap missions, saloons, and flophouses line Third Avenue as well as adjoining streets. Plumped down in the center of this Five Points district is the sober, respectable-looking administration office of the Third Avenue Railway Company. It faces Scratch Park with the ruffled air of an outraged old lady.

We did not linger in the neighborhood. It was almost dark.

"We can stop at the next corner," Mrs. Steinway said. "We haven't covered much ground, but we've seen a lot."

There was more to see, even in the one block. The houses, like those to the south of Scratch Park, were old. Stoops sagged, roofs rippled and broken window panes gaped at us. But this was not what attracted us. The women who leaned out of them caught our interest. They were of the high-yellow variety, young and pretty, most of them, with painted cheeks and lips. Color took the place of clothing.

"Yes," said John Hartmayer, when I asked him about the street a few months later, "that was colored prostitute row. It's been cleaned out now. The building inspector condemned the houses. They've been gutted with fire since then."

Park Avenue has its Scratch Parkites. It also has its cornfields. Mrs. Steinway and I did not linger in the park, but we did stop to see the cornfield.

With poker faces, we marched out of the little square and street of the painted ladies as rapidly as our feet would move into Joe Elder's combination tomato patch and cornfield. It was old Alabama brought North, even to the darky leaning up against the side of a cabin to keep it in place, with a hound dog resting easy at his side.

Joe Elder runs the National Negro Boat Terminal, a large hand-lettered sign on his gatepost tells the world. He lives on a barge that nuzzles against the cornfield—a cornfield that literally climbs the river banks. For decoration, there is a pair of Dresden figures in the tomato patch.

Joe Elder got the idea of starting a cabaret on a boat a few months before we came along. He thought he would make a waterfront Connie's Inn out of his barge. The plan was a good one, but it didn't work.

Instead of attracting sightseeing pleasure-seekers, the National Negro Boat Terminal drew visiting rag-pickers. "Those fellows never work," Policeman John Hartmayer of the Twenty-Fifth Precinct told us. "They like to laze around too much."

The rag-pickers were lazing around when we walked by, darkies of the lean, angular, double-shuffle build. None of them paid any attention to us. Focusing on a new object requires too much exertion.

We drifted over to the edge of a barge, where two negroes of a high-yellow cast sat shaking dice. They looked up indifferently when we exclaimed at sight of the cornfield.

"But this isn't nothin' to what you'll find on Park Avenue round these parts," said the occupant of one of the barges. "Now take that tug up yonder." He pointed in the direction of a boat tied to a Frank L. Burns coal yard dock. "That man was a millionaire. He's lost all his money and's livin' on that thing; why don't you go up and see him? He's got some right on this avenue."

The man who had a right on Park Avenue lived in a tugboat.

"Yes, you'll find him and his family there," the fireman on the William Lawrence fireboat told us. "We've all pitched in and helped keep them together."

The Lewis family home was anchored off the docks of the Burns Brothers coal-yard, at One Hundred and Thirtieth Street and Park Avenue. It had no smokestack, was badly in need of paint, and suggested a barge rather than a brisk little tug. Two tiny children peered at us through holes in the coal yard fence.

"Them kids belong to the Lewises," the fireman said.

"These ladies want to see your boat."

The mother, a plump, black-eyed young woman in beach pajamas, came out of the coal-office door to welcome us. Callers were infrequent. She was glad to see people.

"Yes, we've been living on the tug since last November," she said. "It's our only home." Mr. and Mrs. Lewis were from Florida. They lost everything they had during a hurricane. Because of relatives in New York, they headed north. Things went from bad to worse. Finally, when the threat of eviction came in New York, Mr. Lewis turned to the waterfront for help. He had been brought up with boats. He found a half-submerged tug in the Harlem River near One Hundred and Sixtieth Street. With the aid of the men on the fire-boat, he raised it. They hauled it down to the coal dock. Being handy with carpentering, he fitted it up inside, cleaned out the mud, and put in a stove. His wife and two children moved aboard a week after he dug the tug up.

The afternoon we called, finishing touches were just being put on a new bathroom. An old barge captain had donated the linoleum, somebody else came along with a bathtub, and a wrecking company had furnished the beaver-board walls. Mr. Lewis painted them white with a faint edging of black. The linoleum was black and white.

"I have no money," Mr. Lewis said, "but we've been able to get along pretty well."

He was a slight, harried-looking man, well-educated and nervously eager to be working.

His father lived on the boat also. "I can watch the babies," he said.

"Aren't you afraid the children will fall overboard?" we asked Mrs. Lewis.

"No, I manage to keep an eye on them."

Mrs. Steinway went back several months later with some clothes for the family. She stepped into a tragic scene. One of the babies had fallen overboard. It was dead when the firemen fished it out.

Across the Harlem River from Joe Elder's Negro Boat Terminal is Mott Haven. A congested district it was, as we looked at it, baked in the heat of the summer sun.

Along about 1865, Jordan L. Mott tacked his name to this locality. The elder Mott purchased the lands from Gouveneur Morris, the Patroon, and set up an iron foundry. It was he who dug the canal in the rear of his foundry yard, extending north from the Harlem River for about a fourth of a mile.

They say that others than Mott have explored these waters.

Captain Kidd, the standby of all romance weavers, held forth on the point just beyond Joe Elder's yard. Legend has it that he buried a portion of his treasures here, shot one of his sailors, and stuck him in the trench along with the chests of gold, silver, and precious stones.

When we picked up the thread of our walk at One Hundred and Thirty-Fifth Street and the river, we entered a region of terribly new, uninteresting cubicled buildings that house milk terminals, schools, armories, and even a synagogue. The buildings were monotonously alike. Our contact with the river was shut off by fenced-in car barns and yards.

We were in the doldrums. Not until we swung onto the tag end of Seventh Avenue, did we get out. The Paul Laurence

Dunbar Apartments broke the spell. Rockefeller owns them. Here in these neatly arranged brick blocks of buildings that extend over an entire square, Mr. Rockefeller has made living possible for Harlem's upper-crust in Harlem.

In this serenely calm modern apartment house unvisited as yet by Carl Van Vechten, live the Black Belt's Intelligentsia, among them Mr. and Mrs. Roscoe Conkling Bruce, Senior, who are in charge of the Dunbar Apartments, and their son and daughter-in-law, Mr. and Mrs. Roscoe Conkling Bruce, Jr. The last named is Fannie Hurst's secretary. Paul Robeson and Bill Robinson are also tenants of the Rockefellers.

Life in the Dunbar Apartments is a tale less familiar to those who associate present-day Harlem with Stormy Weather and Ethel Waters at the Cotton Club, or Small's, Tillie's, the Nest, and the Spider Web. It is peaceful, bookish, and conservative. We found Chopin and not Jazz on the Victrola records, de Maupassant on the library shelves, and Quimper china on the dining tables.

The Dunbar is built of tapestry brick around a garden in which grow trees, grass, flowers, and children. The shops are in keeping with the quality air of the block. Among the smartest is that of Madame Walker, the famous negro beauty specialist who amassed a fortune taking the kink out of hair.

Mr. Bruce was at one-time superintendent of several schools in Washington, D. C. He wears a Phi Beta Kappa key. Mrs. Bruce is a large motherly woman with a vast amount of statistical information about Harlem at her fingertips.

"Have you ever heard of the Latch-Key child?" she asked. We had not.

"You see these children very often in the streets of Harlem," she said. "They are little things who wear a string about their necks, with a latch-key tied to it. This means that their mothers are out working and that there is no one at home to look after them. They are at the mercy of whoever runs across them, until night, when their mothers come home. We avoid that trouble in the Dunbar Apartments by having a day nursery."

Mrs. Bruce paused for breath. "And then there is the Lodgers' system. I saw it practiced the other day in a three-room apartment occupied by three families. This meant fourteen people living in three small rooms. They manage it by working the apartment in shifts. As fast as one group gets through sleeping another takes its place.

"This is caused by housing conditions," she continued. "The ideal density in a city is thirty-five people to an acre. In Harlem, we have over three hundred and thirty-six to the acre."

Nineteen

Linen-Duster Days

OUR sixth journey led us past Coogan's Bluffs, now the Polo Grounds, and Rockland Palace, local dance hall of the neighborhood. Both lie in the shadow of the elevated railroad tracks at One Hundred and Fifty-Fifth Street and Eighth Avenue.

James J. Coogan, an Irishman, once Borough President of Manhattan, was the owner of Coogan's Bluffs in the latter part of the nineteenth century. Then the bluffs furnished pasturage for goats and land for squatters.

Mr. Coogan and his wife believed in the acquisition of real estate. Much of the property around town today bears the name of Coogan. For example, the five-story loft building on the northeast corner of Twenty-Sixth Street and Sixth Avenue. At the time the Coogan's built it, the structure was the tallest in that section of New York. People came from miles around to observe the skyline of the city from the roof of Coogan's building. Mr. Coogan has been dead for many years. His widow owns the Twenty-Sixth Street property. The bluffs, however, are no longer controlled by the family. The Polo Grounds Association has acquired them. They say that more famous baseball and football games have been played on its green than in any other amusement park in the world.

Rockland Palace is the setting for Bohemian dances. Greenwich Village parties are staged here. It is a strange, slightly gloomy, old-fashioned place. On the hot July morning that Mrs. Steinway and I explored it, the dim musty interior felt refreshingly cool. A tall West Indian negro guarded the door. He could tell us little of its history, save that Rockland Palace had been there as far back as he could remember.

I learned more about it, in Stewart's Cafeteria on Sheridan Square down in the Village, than I did from the management in Harlem.

A boy who was passing out notices of a costume ball handed me one. The dance was being staged in Rockland Palace.

"Why are you picking on Rockland Palace for your party?" I asked.

"Oh, we've been going up there for years," he said. "All the drags are held in it."

So are Marathon dances, for colored and white people. Built originally for the fashionable balls of Harlem, the old Rockland Palace takes what it can get today.

The distance between the Polo Grounds and the Speedway

is uninteresting. After we left Rockland Palace, there was little for us to explore until we reached the celebrated old trotting horse highway. The Interborough railroad yards barred us from the river.

"Let's see if we can't cut through," Mrs. Steinway suggested.

In spite of a "No Admittance" sign, we stepped bravely into the machine-strewn yards. It was the first week in July. A blazing sun beat down on our heads. Its rays flashed back at us from the steel rails. I lost two pounds on that walk. The going was good until we reached the end of the yards.

"You ladies can't go on here," an old Interborough watchman shouted. "Ye've got to turn back!"

We fussed and fumed. Turning back meant retracing our way for ten blocks.

"Oh, Pat, have a heart! Let them girls through," called a track-man. "Take them up to the Speedway."

Grumbling about women in general and us in particular, he finally relented.

"I'll let ye out this time, but I never want to see yer faces round here again!" he shouted, brandishing a stick in our faces.

"You won't," we promised, waving goodbye as we headed north on the historic Speedway, a highway that touched the peak in the latter half of the nineteenth century, when trotting horses were a millionaire's hobby.

From around 1880 to 1908, the Speedway was thronged with little sulkys driven by nifty gentlemen sporting burnsides and broad-brimmed gray felt hats.

Hugh J. Connolly, proprietor of the old Office Tavern at 1439 Third Avenue, has likenesses of all the old boys hanging in his lobby. They are assembled in a picture painted by a man named Rosenbaum. I think Knoedler, the art dealer, was responsible for the commission.

Though the name key has been lost, there are many faces in the painting that are easily recognizable. Among them James R. Keene, E. E. Smathers, Nathan Straus, and Michael Reid.

The Office Tavern used to be the meeting-place of these trotting-horse fans, after a spin up the Speedway and back. Mr. Connolly is constantly turning down offers for his Speedway picture.

"Most of those men were my customers," he explained. "I'd as soon sell a picture of my family."

Our half-way house was the old Richard F. Carman mansion at One Hundred and Seventy-Fifth Street and the Harlem River. It is a curious, framed, gable-roofed building, suggestive of the former grandeur that clings to the side of the Heights. The Department of Parks owns it now.

Carman was a real-estate magnate who flourished in Civil War days. At one time he owned the building now the property of India House. At his death, he was said to be worth eight million dollars.

Reginald Pelham Bolton, in his history of Washington Heights, says that an imposing white marble shaft marks the graves of Carman and his family in Trinity Cemetery on One Hundred and Fifty-Third Street near the Hudson.

"The present condition of the memorial," writes Mr. Bolton, "is evidence of the neglect that is shown to the memory of men, who at one time have been prominent by reason of their acquisition of money or property."

There are so many places in New York where I would like to live for a while. Each one has a character of its own. I have often thought of spending the week-end at Sweet's Hotel on Fulton Street and the waterfront. Of all the river hotels I know, this is the only one that has kept its original seafaring atmosphere with the few old clipper-ship captains still making it their port of call.

Another section I would like to relive is the Speedway. It is closely linked with my childhood days, because of a friend of our family, Michael Reid, trotting-horse fan, whose picture hangs in the Office Tavern.

It was Mr. Reid's custom during the season to drive each day through Central Park, up to the Speedway. I was usually tucked in the buggy too. As soon as Black Raven, Mr. Reid's favorite horse, hit the Speedway, he struck his gait. As if on the wings of the wind, we would race the length of the highway. One of our guideposts was the Carman mansion.

Perched high up on the cliffs, the homely ornate Victorian residence is distinctive enough to be preserved. I wish that the city might convert it into a museum of the period which it emulates.

At present, the Department of Parks uses it not only for offices but as a small source of revenue. The upper floors are divided into apartments which rent by the month. We rested for a while on the front steps of the Carman house. The main entrance faces west and the heights. The back porch overlooks the Harlem River. I imagine that the trees which shade the old-fashioned heart-shaped drive, are those planted by the Carmans and that the landscaping of the grounds remains much as it did when they occupied the house. The interior has not been changed. The same elaborately carved white and black mantel-piece, high ceilings, minutely designed frescoes, and winding staircases are there. The only difference perhaps is the painting of the fine walnut woodwork. In the original, it must have been very beautiful.

The former Carman home can easily be seen from the Speed-way. It is reached by a steep and winding road, just beyond High Bridge. This particular bridge which spans the Harlem River was originally known as Aqueduct Bridge and at the time of its construction in 1848, considered one of the most famous in the United States.

Edgar Allan Poe used to pace back and forth on it, gazing moodily down upon the water far below. They say that many of his poems were composed here.

If he had been with us that hot July day he might have been moved to spin a poem around the magnificent yachts at anchor in the ship basins across from the Speedway at One Hundred and Ninety-Second Street.

"Them's rum-runners that was," explained a boatman in one of the local boat clubs that fringe the Harlem River. "Ye'll find a good many famous yachts there. If you go over they might show them to ye."

"We'll wait for cooler weather," I said.

Twenty

⚶

Rowboat Club Row

JESS' SWEET POTATO
PATCH AT 207TH ST.
AND THE HARLEM RIVER.

THE upper section of Manhattan Island is rich in neighborhood types. Those on the Harlem River front are of a nautical turn of mind, particularly the old boys who bask in the brilliant autumn sunlight on the "decks" of the little boat clubs that edge the water in the region between One Hundred and Ninety-Second and Two Hundredth Streets, just below the Speedway.

The clubs had their heyday when towing on the Harlem River was a summer pastime.

One of them, the Atalantis, at One Hundred and Ninety-Sixth Street and the Speedway, dates back to 1848. William

Moran is the Commodore and Ike Halloway the oldest member. He's been coming to the club for fifty years.

Across the river from the Atalantis is the Consolidated Ship-building Corporation, with yachts in the yards belonging to the Woolworths, the Curtises, and, they say, a Vanderbilt.

Some of the boats in this vicinity were painted gray for rum-running purposes, or camouflaged in zigzag stripes of black and white. Many were stripped to the decks for action. But men along the shore told me that a couple of weeks before repeal, all rum-running boats were taken out of active service. The repeal of the Eighteenth Amendment sent bootleggers' craft to drydock.

I know of another famous yacht base, where thirty-five toys —the playthings of millionaires, baubles of the wealthy—lie at anchor in Tebo Basin, off the Brooklyn Flats.

Hooded and blanketed, like so many spirited thoroughbreds, the luxurious boats chafe back and forth against the docks— eager to be nosing their course through the salt spray of sound and ocean. Stacked up against the cost of running them, their board and keep in the Basin amounts to nothing.

Seventy-five dollars a month ensures the best of craft a comfortable berth and care. Which is all very well, but take the same boat out for a week-end cruise and see what it costs.

There is a pioneer flavor to waterfront homes. The early American spirit that fired our people to frontier lives has popped out in the rustic river abodes of the Harlem section.

Behind the Esso gasoline filling station, at Two Hundredth Street and the Speedway, we discovered a house on wheels.

The little wooden structure was painted a bright green, gay awnings shaded the windows and morning-glory vines had been trained up over a wooden frame that shielded the hood. The house had been parked there for a year.

A Mr. and Mrs. Peterson lived in it. He worked in New York. As long as his job lasted, he was going to stay in town.

The Esso filling station is built on the site of the old Durando Hotel, a half-way house famous in linen-duster days when the Speedway was crowded with trotting-horse fans.

A curiously individual group they are, these houseboat homes. The personal taste of the people who live in them is reflected in the shape, ornamentations, and furnishings of the houseboats. All had porches, many flowers, and one boasted a stained-glass dining-room window.

A houseboat costs about eight hundred dollars. Ten dollars a month is the docking charge. The majority have telephones, electricity, and water from the city.

Year in and year out these boats anchor off Two Hundred and Seventh Street. All have names. *Sunny* is printed on the life preserver of John Olsen's boat, and *Jennie's House* appears on the side of a neighbor's dwelling. Sailors' handiwork in the form of rope-knotted curtains, carved frames, and silk-embroidered flags dress up the rooms.

Jess Thomas is the guardian angel of the houseboat settlement. He is a great, tall, blue-black Negro from Binnettsville, South Carolina, with a friendly smile and a pride in his neighborhood. He reminded me of the descendants of the African chieftains who live on Edisto Island off the coast of South Carolina.

It is Jess's sweet potato patch and peanut crop that has made a farming community of this locality in a city of six million.

"Shucks, they told me peanuts and sweet potatoes can't be

grown up here!" he chuckled. "But look at 'em." He pointed to the healthy plants. "After frost hits the vines I'll be able to dig 'em."

When the children of the neighborhood told their school teacher that Jess had raised sweet potatoes and peanuts she doubted them.

Jess sent her some peanuts and potatoes last year to prove the story. She's going to get some this year. "I got the seeds from my home state," Jess explained to us.

Jess's tastes also run to landscape gardening. Neatly planned paths lead to his little lilac-shaded home. Quaint old bits of statuary decorate the rock garden on which he is working. "I found that on the junk pile," he said, looking at a funny Victorian iron figure. He whitewashed it and placed it above a fountain arrangement in the community courtyard.

We spent most of the morning in the houseboat community, talking to the neighbors, visiting with Jess and dawdling along the waterfront.

It was the start of our seventh walk—early in October. The day was warm and sunny, the little gardens bright with flowers and there was a touch of Indian summer in the air.

There is a slight bend in the river at Two Hundred and Seventh Street. It forms a cove that is ideal for houseboats. To the right is the University Heights Bridge, beyond lies the Board of Transportation Yard.

"It's sheltered in the winter too," Mrs. Olsen said. "I don't have to bring in my rubber plant until late November."

With reluctance we left the little settlement, skirting the Board of Transportation Yard until we reached Two Hundred and Fifteenth Street. There we had to turn inland. Five blocks away lay the end of Manhattan Island. To reach it we detoured by way of Isham Park.

ABOVE THE HUDSON ON THE
HEIGHTS

"You will find much that is interesting, in that end of town," Rudolph Pfortner, an old New Yorker, had told me. We did. The first point of interest was the only farm in New York. It covers more than an acre of ground and is owned by a Mr. Fellman, who lives in New Orleans.

Jess Thomas's sweet potato patch was the nearest thing to it. But this went him one better. There were golden pumpkins in the field!

"This is a strange thing in New York," Mrs. Steinway said. "Let's go over and see what it's all about."

We crossed beneath the elevated train viaduct and entered the yard at the side gate. Wooden tables backed up against the walls of an old farmhouse were stacked high with ripening squash, great yellow pumpkins, and red tomatoes. A man was in the field hoeing. I stepped across a bean patch to him.

"Tell me something about your house."

He shook his head, dropped the hoe, and ran indoors.

Presently a woman came out. "No stories, no stories," she yelled. "Every time the papers say this only farm in New York, man raises rent."

Twenty-One

Museum Pieces

SUMMER HOUSE ON OLD SEAMAN ESTATE

DIRECTLY across the street from the only farm in New York City, rise the grassy slopes of Isham Park.

This was originally the Bouwery of Tobias Teunissen, a native of Nieuw Haarlem. Sky-reaching, cubicled apartment buildings have obliterated all trace of pastoral memories, save the little plot now farmed by Italians, and the hill where the Isham mansion stands.

The Isham estate was not very large. It consisted of some twenty or thirty acres running from Two Hundred and Eleventh Street north to Spuyten Duyvil Creek.

In 1860, the land came into the possession of the Ferrises who built a big house on top of the hill. William B. Isham bought it and the land from the Ferrises in 1864. He lived there until his death, when his daughter, Julia Isham Taylor, gave the estate to the City of New York for a public park.

We climbed the hill and explored the old house. It is a curious place, built at an angle, with a huge circular hall in the center and big rooms opening off at various corners. The drawing room is occupied by the Washington Heights branch of the Daughters of the American Revolution. The other rooms on the same floor are given over to Department of Parks offices, while the upper floor has been converted into apartments.

From the side porch of the Isham home, it is possible to catch a glimpse of Marble Mansion, the oldest house in the neighborhood.

The approach to Marble House was through a mass of tangled weeds. A distant view of stately white pillars and a quaint wooden well lured us on. Thistles and burrs clung to our skirts as we made our way up the hill.

Doors were locked, windows closed tight. There was not a sign of life about the place. We walked through the grounds, enjoyed the magnificent view both of the Hudson and the Harlem Rivers, studied ancient bits of statuary that dotted the once ornately landscaped terrace, and then with fear and trembling rang a bell at the side entrance beneath a huge, crumbling porte-cochere.

Not a sound came from the house. We waited. Finally, the forbidding old black-walnut carved door opened a tiny crack and the face of a little Irish woman appeared.

"What is it ye be wanting?" she asked.

"Could you tell us something of the history of the house?" we ventured.

"I couldn't do that." She shook her head. "Ye'll have to ask Mr. Dwyer. He's down in the marble arch."

She pointed to what seemed to be the top of a stone structure that looked not unlike the Washington Arch on Washington Square. Shacks and old buildings clung to its sides like so many barnacles. "The entrance is through them iron gates," the maid explained.

We spent some ten minutes exploring the ancient marble arch where Mr. Dwyer was hidden. To find him we went through the iron gates into empty rooms and climbed a corkscrew stair that shot up a dark and musty corridor. His lair was at the top, in the offices of the Marble Arch Company, contractors and builders.

James Dwyer belongs to the New York in which lived Ridley, the old merchant; Richard Croker, the Tammany politician, and Michael Reid, the trotting-horse fan.

He was sitting at the top of the steps in front of an old walnut table when we cornered him.

"And what do ye be after?" he demanded as we climbed into his office.

"We're very much interested in the history of your house," I said. "It's a beautiful old place."

He rested a heavy blackthorn cane across the top of his table, pushed his derby back on his head, and leaned forward. "There's not much to tell," he spoke reluctantly. "I've had it twenty-six years. They say it was built eighty or a hundred years ago." He toyed with a massive gold chain stretched across an old-fashioned waistcoat. The red of his necktie was matched by a red rose in the lapel of his coat. "I'm a contractor. I built the Soldiers and Sailors Monument, the Metropolitan Museum of Art and remodeled Castle Garden into the Aquarium. The house is likely to come down before long.

"Could we go in it?" There was hesitation in our question. None too enthusiastically he called a workman to take us to the roof of Marble Mansion so that we might get the full benefit of the view.

Our inspection was brief. The great halls, huge drawing room, the library, the ancient attic, and immense kitchen suggested some southern plantation. They were filled with heavy walnut and mahogany furniture.

The land on which Marble House stands was purchased by John Seaman, the son of Dr. Valentine Seaman, an eighteenth-century physician. It is built of local marble quarried on the property. The grounds of the estate were once laid out with charming walks and shrubbery and adorned with arches and statuary brought from France. The imposing marble archway where Mr. Dwyer has his office was the entrance that led to it. Famous balls, elaborate parties, and great people held forth in this now gloomy and silent house.

Over the elaborately carved mantelpiece in the dining room of Marble House hangs a large photograph of the estate taken thirty years ago. Mr. Dwyer is standing in the doorway. With a silk hat, top coat, and Van Dyke beard he presents an important figure. Then the grounds were carefully landscaped, the blue limestone walk nicely smoothed and the shrubbery neatly trimmed.

THE OLD SEAMAN HOUSE
217½ ST. WEST OF BROADWAY

I'm afraid the clock stopped for Marble Mansion then. Today it is a ghostly figure beckoning out of the past.

The tapestried curtains veil broken drawing-room windows, wide cracks in the huge front doors, let in cold river winds, and dust covers the balustrades of the grand stairway.

Mrs. Charles MacLean, daughter of the elder Jordan Mott, who founded Mott Haven, tells me that Marble Mansion was considered the most beautiful house in Harlem when she was a girl.

The early architecture of Marble Mansion has been rather disfigured by a square tower that replaced the original dome. Mr. Dwyer put it up when he built in a swimming pool on the third floor. The pool has never been used, nor has the tower.

The day we visited Mr. Dwyer, he had a plan afoot to turn all of the Marble Mansion property into a new housing scheme. If this goes through, the ancient house will be torn down before this book is published.

It is the last of the old-timers on Manhattan Island. In just such a mansion, the first families of Old New York must have bowed their way through the minuet, drunk toasts to the New World, and faced the difficulties as well as the pleasures of life.

That they lived comfortably and enjoyed the luxuries of a sophisticated existence is shown in the remains of a great conservatory at the south side of the house, the eighteenth-century French statuary that dots the grounds, and the elaborate coach houses now converted into apartments at the far end of the land.

From our crow's-nest climb to the tower of Marble House, we looked north to the end of Manhattan Island, now separated from the mother island by the Harlem Ship Canal. Baker's Field flanks it on the south.

ANTIQUE FRENCH
STATUE ON SEAMAN ESTATE

Twenty-Two

The End of the Island

A RIVERFRONT DINER.

"Do you suppose we can follow the waterfront along the Canal?" Ruth Steinway asked.

"We can try," I replied. "But first, let's have something to eat, I'm starved."

As usual, we ate in a diner, our favorite waterfront restaurant. This one happened to be a few blocks from the Harlem Ship Canal. It stood alongside Mr. Dwyer's marble arch, on Broadway, at Two Hundred and Eighteenth Street.

Freshly tubbed box trees, murals of Tyrolean flavor, and a long clean white-tiled counter lured us in.

"What'll you have?" sang out the husky proprietor.

"Two hamburgers on rye and a couple of glasses of beer," I answered.

"Make it two Johnnies and schooners," repeated the proprietor to himself. He looked like an ex-prizefighter. They tell me that prize fighters back the diners. Some own chains of glittering food cars. The diners run into money. Few individual restaurant keepers have the cash to buy them.

Diners seldom vary in appearance. There is the usual highly painted exterior, sometimes trimmed with chromium plate, the steps at either end that have replaced wheels, the numerous windows cut to resemble railroad diners, and the inevitable railway car top, with little ventilators and a slightly sloping roof.

Sometimes there are tables for ladies arranged opposite the big counter. We preferred sitting on the stools at the counter. It's much more like having a front-row seat. We liked to watch the hamburger being fried, see the big nickel coffee pot bubbling, and give the pies and cakes the once-over.

It was half past one when we left the diner and headed for the ship canal.

'I think we can go a good bit along the Hudson before the afternoon is over," said Mrs. Steinway.

"If we can cut through Baker's Field, it will be possible," I said. "Otherwise, I don't believe we'll get much beyond Inwood."

We headed up Broadway to the water. The street is overshadowed by the West Side subway, which comes above ground a few blocks before it crosses the canal.

Beyond our diner lay Baker's Field. The property now owned by Columbia University was once a great estate. It belonged to Isaac Michael Dyckman, a descendant of the famous Dyckman farm family. He built it in 1867 as a wedding present for his bride. The Isaac Dyckmans had two children, Mary Alice and Fannie Fredericka Dyckman. They were born in the old-fashioned brown mansard-roofed house. As little girls, they played on the green lawns that surrounded it.

"Though we never went very near the water," Fannie Fredericka, now Mrs. Alexander McMillan Welch of 15 East Seventy-First Street, told me. "We lived in the house until 1904," she continued. "Father died in 1899. But Mother stayed on, five years."

Mary Alice married Bashford Dean, Columbia professor, trustee of the American Museum of Natural History, and curator of armor at the Metropolitan Museum of Art. He died in 1928.

Mrs. Welch's husband is the first vice president of the New York Savings Bank.

After the Dyckmans sold the old house, it passed through many hands, until ten or twelve years ago, when the late George F. Baker, the banker, bought the property and presented it to Columbia. The football field is named after the financier.

The manor-house is used for quartering the teams and crews during the football and racing season. There are some twenty-eight acres in the property which extends along the Harlem shipping canal from Broadway to Tubby's Hook.

Our way through Baker's Field was barred by high wire fences that extended to the water's edge. There was no possibility of scaling them.

"We might walk back and go through the grounds," I suggested.

But this way, too, was discouraged by great gates.

"Perhaps there is a chance of reaching the canal through the opposite end," Ruth Steinway said.

We turned up West Two Hundred and Eighteenth Street, skirting the Columbia land as we went, and always keeping an eye on the winding ship canal. We walked in at the main gate to Baker's Field, taking the cinder driveway that led to the stadium. The grounds were beautiful. There are some nice old trees to shade the drive. The last of the autumn flowers were blooming, gardeners were at work sprucing them up for Saturday and a football game. A crew of men was busy putting the field in shape. They paid no attention to us, as we cut cross lots to the water. Again a high fence stopped us.

"There's no use trying to get any place here," Mrs. Steinway said, "the fence extends round."

We turned back, taking a new path. It led us to locked gates.

"If we can't get through here, we'll have to go all the way back to the other end of the field," I wailed.

"What about crawling under the gates?" ventured Mrs. Steinway.

Others had evidently tried. There was a little hollow beneath the gates. We shoved our bags and cameras through and then rolled under ourselves. Just as we were halfway out a large and impressive limousine sailed by. The astonished occupants stared in amazement at our reclining figures. They were still looking back when we climbed out and up to the sidewalk.

West Two Hundred and Eighteenth Street extends to the waterfront. It terminated in a little cove. To the right on the canal's edge lies the white-brick early-American crew house presented by the late Mr. Edwin Gould to Columbia. It is here in the early spring that the crack oarsmen of Columbia practice for the river races held later in the season.

The United States or Harlem River Ship Canal which now marks the end of Manhattan Island winds even more picturesquely than the little Spuyten Duyvil Creek that once served as the boundary-line of Manhattan Island.

This canal cuts through the rocks that once formed part of the old Dyckman estate.

The real end of Manhattan Island is Marble Hill; it extends from Two Hundred and Twenty-Fourth to Two Hundred and Thirtieth Streets. They say it was about 1895 that it was separated from the main island by the canal, though it is still part of the Borough of Manhattan. It is around Marble Hill that the little Spuyten Duyvil Creek circled.

Twenty-Three

❧

An Indian Touch

HOME OF INDIAN PRINCESS
ON HARLEM SHIP CANAL

INWOOD PARK is lonely. There was an eerie quality in the atmosphere the October afternoon we took the river road that skirts it.

The stillness that sometimes comes late in the fall, when the last little summer insects have stopped chirping, hung over the gold and scarlet-flecked autumn landscape.

The bright sunlight accented the loneliness of the scene. Perhaps it is because the past is greater than the present that a sense of the unseen persists on Inwood Hill. Formal estates once stretched their landscaped length over their slopes. Famous men visited its homes, and celebrated families owned them.

Inwood has had its scars. The gloomy House of the Good

Shepherd cut a jagged cross upon its soil. Hidden in a grove of sinister pines, the jail-like brick building that imprisoned New York's wayward girls offered a strange contrast to the wealthy estates surrounding it.

The institution moved years ago. Winter storms and summer heat have gradually worn down the shell of the grim structure. The day we circled Inwood, the remains of the House of the Good Shepherd were being torn down. It stood up the hill, on another road. But its turrets were visible from our path.

The early history of Inwood is fascinating. Its little coves, sunny slopes, and protected hollows offered a first-rate camping ground for the Indians. They held their campfire circles about the huge tulip trees. They buried their dead in the shell beds that are still being uncovered at Inwood.

If you are interested in the Indian pageant that swept across Inwood Hill, visit the Museum of the American Indian at One Hundred and Fifty-Third Street and Broadway. John Heye is the curator. With the aid of Reginald Pelham Bolton, who uncovered many of the Indian shell beds, Mr. Heye has assembled a fine panorama of Indian life on the upper end of Manhattan Island.

Mr. and Mrs. Harry Voorhees also keep alive the Indian tradition of Inwood. They make pottery. Much of it is of Indian design.

They live in a small white frame house more than a century old. It was built for a retired sea captain seeking a snug harbor.

"We have never been able to find out his name," Mr. Voorhees said, "but Pop Seeley told us stories about him. Pop lived here until he died. We got the house from him."

It is a quaint, cheery little place with latticed windows and a snug quality. Oil lamps, coal stoves, and open fires lend rural atmosphere. Back of it are the studios where the Inwood pottery is made. The clay used for the Indian bowls comes from the hills roundabout.

Both Mr. and Mrs. Voorhees mold the pottery and give instruction in the making of it. The public school teachers often come to the Inwood Studios for class work.

It is a romantic spot and a unique one in which to study. Near Mr. and Mrs. Voorhees' home is the cove where the striped bass bite. The beach was crowded with fishermen angling for bass. One man we saw had just caught a fish sixteen inches long. It was his third that afternoon.

Reginald Pelham Bolton says that most of the land along these waters, including the Isham and Seaman estates, was originally owned by Tobias Tuenissen, farm assistant to Dr. de la Montagne, first settler in the New Harlem district, in 1636.

On the ship canal, just beyond the Voorhees' home, is the little red-frame house where the Cherokee Indian woman lives with her son, Chief White Rock, and his family.

The Indian woman's home is shaded by a great tulip tree credited with being the oldest on Manhattan Island. On our walk that afternoon through Inwood Park, we saw many ancient tulip trees.

They say that just below the Indian house has always been a good point for fishing off Manhattan Island, and that because of the excellent quality of the catch, human beings, from the Indians down, have always lived here. The warm sunny autumn afternoon that Mrs. Steinway and I crossed the white sands of the little cove, men with fishing poles were busy casting, as they had in the past, for striped bass.

The cove on the Hudson River side of the canal is spoken of geographically as "Tubby's Hook." The surrounding woods belonged to the Dyckman family. During the nineteenth and early part of the twentieth century, substantial residential houses were built on this land, later to be known as Inwood Hill Park. The main road that intersected it was called Bolton Road, after one of the old Washington Heights families. The lower or river road ran from Tubby Hook along the Hudson to a point just above Dyckman Street and Two Hundred and Seventh. This was the road that Mrs. Steinway and I took.

In crossing from the Harlem to the Hudson River, we followed the ship canal. Spuyten Duyvil Creek, which extended a few blocks farther up, is now almost obliterated. In recent years this bubbling little stream, over which in winter the neighborhood children skated, has practically disappeared. It marked the real boundary line of the upper end of Manhattan Island.

The inhabitants of Marble Hill, which flanks the north side of the ship canal, often win bets on their location. The majority of people do not know that Marble Hill is a part of Manhattan Island.

Twenty-Four

A Deserted Village

FISHING ON
NORTH RIVER DOCK

A MAN who had just bran-
dished an upraised ax, and
given chase to a scurrying little fellow, with coat-tails fly-
ing, took us back to B. E. F. village at Dyckman Street and the
Hudson River after our Inwood walk.

We were nearing the stopping point of our seventh adventure when we happened on the drama in pantomime. Nothing
could have been more peaceful than the winding river road we
had taken.

"It's difficult to realize that we are really in New York City,"
Mrs. Steinway said; "no people, no noise and no excitement."

We paused to enjoy the lazy autumn afternoon, bright with
golden sunshine and changing foliage. To our left were the sloping Inwood hills, to the right, the Hudson stretched a silvery

ribbon beneath the Jersey cliffs. Below a straggling settlement of shacks and lean-tos fringed the water.

A man swinging an ax hacked at a wood pile near a house. We watched him with idle interest. A short distance away stood a soda-pop stand tended by a ragged-aproned proprietor.

Suddenly the wood-cutter stopped, gave a shout, picked up his ax, and charged at the soda stand owner, who dived out from his store like a frightened rabbit and scuttled down the shore-line to a small hut. He locked himself in just as the man with the ax arrived. After hanging around for a few minutes the big fellow went back to his wood-chopping.

"What is that settlement over there?" we asked at Captain R. T. Windle's boat shop when we reached Dyckman Street.

"Used to be a B. E. F. village," someone volunteered. "It ain't much of anything now. Why don't you walk up and take a look at it?"

We followed the shore, climbing over the cans, rocks, and refuse to the wind-swept group of shacks. A man and a dog guarded the first one, the same man who had wielded the ax. He stared at us through surly eyes but called to his dog to be quiet when it barked. Just beyond his house was a small tar-papered hut marked headquarters. From the top of it waved a tattered American flag and posted up on the front in bold letters was this verse:

> "Hoover was the Engineer
> Mellon rang the bell
> Wall Street gave the signal
> Then the country went to Hell."

"What was the fight all about?" we asked the soda-pop man.

"My name Joseph," he explained. "Crazy Harry, he chase me with ax. I had hammer but run to get club!"

"Are you afraid of him?"

"Naw, just have to hurry when he comes with ax."

"Is this still a B. E. F. town?"

Joseph shook his head. "No more. Harry and headquarters all that's left. Others move down to Seventy-Fifth Street and Riverside Drive. More millionaires there to help them. Here nothing but woods." He waved an arm in the direction of Inwood Park.

"No," said Captain R. T. Windle, pushing his skipper's hat back on his head. "The trouble with them New Yorkers inland is that they don't know anything 'bout us up here."

We were back again in Captain Windle's shipyard to get neighborhood news.

"We're all fightin' hard for two things in these parts," Captain Windle continued, "and I tell you it's up-hill work. First of all we want a harbor for small boats where they can dock. Do you know that there isn't one in the whole of New York?" He led the way into his sitting room and office. "I'll show you the plan we've had made," pointing to a huge wall-map. "I'm the president of the Hudson River Reclamation Association, that's workin' on this now."

The Captain handed me a blue pamphlet. "This is what we're aiming at." He ran a forefinger down the list of proposed suggestions. "Better boating conditions, cleaner waterways, disposal of driftwood, creation of waterfront parkways, landing floats, and community club-houses, encouragement of water sports and, in general, to make the river-front a pleasure spot instead of an eyesore."

The Captain is right. The New York shoreline of the Hudson River is a mess. Only at two points in our walk along the West-Side waterfront from the Harlem Ship Canal to One Hundred and Forty-Fifth Street have Mrs. Steinway and I found a spot where the natural beauty of the land and river had half a chance. The first is at Inwood Park and the second is a promontory beneath the George Washington Bridge.

R. T. Windle's shipyard has charm. There is a gravel driveway, flowers, a small, low, rambling little frame house where he lives, and all sorts of odds and ends in front—a well, for example, that he works on during the winter months. It's a rustic affair without a drop of water any place near it.

"Not that it matters," said the Captain; "we have a spring." He held up a large, rusty iron automobile spring.

Another object of interest and amusement in the yard is a curious-looking blue boat mounted on something that looks like airplane wings.

"What's that?" we asked.

"An experiment," said the Captain. "A fellow comes up here every Sunday and works on it. He's foreman in a piano factory. They say he's trying to get more speed out o' the boat. But 'bout all he does is take it apart."

To the left of Captain Windle's boatyard lies the Dyckman Street Ferry. The new Washington Bridge has nicked its motor-car trade. Before the bridge was built, Jersey-bound motorists used the ferry constantly.

The docks surrounding the old ferry house are a favorite stomping-ground of local fishermen. Numerous clubs meet on the worn wooden wharves. They cast for anything that comes along. Lafayettes, small minnow-like fish, are the customary catch. Quaint little booths stocked with fishing tackle line the streets leading away from the ferry.

The anglers dig for their bait on Inwood and Convent Hill. Old spades, stuck beneath convenient bushes are cached away, until they are needed, for worm-digging.

Dyckman Street is a wide thoroughfare. In the vicinity of the ferry, it is but little settled. The railroad station, where the Dolly Varden Commuters' train used to stop, is no longer used. There is a charm to the wooded hills that flank it on the water-front, but farther inland it becomes one of the most prosaic crosstown streets in Manhattan. Matter-of-fact drab-looking apartment-houses rise in ungainly rows, along it. Chain stores, delicatessens, and vegetable stalls obliterate all traces of the old Dyckman farm.

Fortunately, the Dyckman homestead has been preserved. The ghosts of Dyckman House must be a very happy lot. The farm-house at Two Hundred and Fourth Street and Broadway where they passed this life has been restored to its former beauty. Even William and Jacobus Dyckman's rooms are said to look much as they did when these hardy pioneers occupied them. Isaac Dyckman, who was born in 1813, lived with his uncles in their old home at Two Hundred and Fourth Street until his marriage. It was his two granddaughters, Mrs. Dean and Mrs. Welch, who presented the Dyckman farm to the City of New York, completely restored, and filled it with family furniture.

Mr. and Mrs. Dean and Mr. and Mrs. Welch advertised the country round for Dyckman family furniture, to put in the house, Reginald Pelham Bolton told me, with the result that every room in the Dyckman farmhouse is filled with authentic pieces, that were in most instances, the original ones used in the home.

The Deans and the Welches themselves worked in arranging and placing it.

Mr. Bolton and his wife set up the relics that he and William L. Calver dug up on Washington Heights. They include belts, buttons, and firearms used by the British, Hessian, and American troops during the Revolutionary War, old pieces of china, and portions of the huts in which the soldiers lived. Some were on the Dyckman farm.

Twenty-Five

The Cloisters and the Nuns

WEST'S BOAT CLUB LANDING
204ᵗʰ ST. AND THE NORTH RIVER

JUST above Captain Windle's shipyard rise Washington Heights. Dyckman Street divides them. To the north is Inwood Park. To the south, on the hill where George Grey Barnard, the sculptor, lives, is the building known as "The Cloisters."

His hill marks the last stand of detached houses in New York. The C. K. G. Billings home was once here, a great estate with wooded slopes, private stables, and landscaped gardens. John D. Rockefeller, Jr., purchased it, along with much of the other land on the hill. It is now being made into a park, just as Inwood has.

They say that in time Mr. Barnard's property will also be a portion of this river-heights park. However, he hopes to continue living in his picturesque home. When Christmas comes around George Grey Barnard misses Caruso. The great tenor used to sing for the famous sculptor on Christmas Eve. The walls of the Cloisters echoed once a year to the golden tones of the Italian singer.

The setting was perfect. Mr. Barnard spent years in Europe acquiring ecclesiastical objects of art that fill the charming old structure on Fort Washington Avenue between One Hundred and Ninetieth and One Hundred and Ninety-First Streets. The interior is peopled with ancient statues of the Virgin Mary, quaint figures of the apostles, as well as altarpieces and elaborately carved choir stalls.

From the windows of his own home, Mr. Barnard can gaze out upon the Cloisters, just across the garden. He loves the building, and he loves the medieval sculpture it contains. He also loves the neighborhood. For thirty-five years he has lived in it.

As a young man, Mr. Barnard came with his bride to the old Nolan house a few blocks down from his present home. His work developed. He needed more space—the impressive residence in which Mr. and Mrs. Barnard now live was built.

The house is strangely reminiscent of Florence. Those who visit it might well be stepping into a Medici palace. The approach on the first floor is down a stone passageway and through grilled-iron doors that open into a lower hall. Up from this rises a staircase balustraded by carved stone.

"That staircase is from the home of Henry Marquand," Mr. Barnard explained, "first president of the Metropolitan Museum of Art." It leads to a vast room that stretches the length of the house—a room with high ceilings, a great medieval fireplace, and rich hangings.

At the far end is a refectory table on which the meals are served.

Near the Cloisters and George Grey Barnard, is the Home of the Poor Clares on Haven Avenue near One Hundred and Eighty-First Street.

The rooftop of the silent gray house in which the Clares live may be seen from the river's edge. Its shuttered windows, deserted porches, and lonely grounds command a superb view of the Hudson, as well as, the new Washington Bridge.

The thirteen women who are passing solitary years in the great mansion at One Hundred and Eighty-First Street and Haven Avenue, belong to the severest of all Catholic orders.

One of them, Lucile Begg, was a debutante of a few seasons back. She joined the Order of the Poor Clares three years ago. The chief vow is that of voluntary silence.

We stared up at the house, as we skirted the water's edge far below. The place is easily distinguishable because of its tight closed shutters, the great trees that shade it, and the fact that it is flanked on either side by towering apartment buildings.

A few hundred yards to the north rise the stone walls of Dr. John Paterno's castle. The Paternos are Italian. The family is responsible for many of the larger apartment houses in town. The Castle is their idea of a fine home. It is imposing, what with turrets, pergolas, orchid houses, conservatories, and swimming pools.

Haven Avenue, the street upon which the Poor Clares and

Doctor Paterno live, was named after the Havens—an old Washington Heights family.

Twenty-Six

◈

River Characters

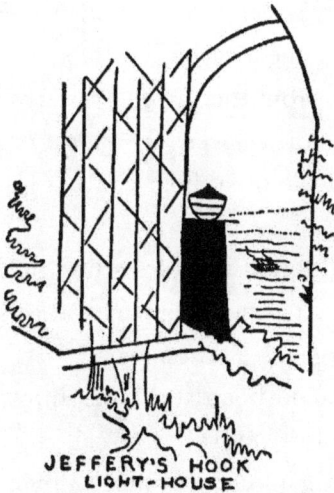

JEFFERY'S HOOK
LIGHT-HOUSE

FOR all suggestions of a city, we might have been miles removed from New York, the morning we started on our seventh walk. It began at Two Hundred and Seventh Street, led past the boat clubs, curved out over rocks to Washington Point, circled beneath Washington Bridge, wound its way over more rocks, down cinder paths to Rum-Boat Row.

There must be fifty or sixty little frame detached houses edging the lane that extends from Two Hundred and Seventh Street to One Hundred and Forty-Fifth Street. Every house is a boat club. They are two-story affairs, built of frame and more or less nondescript in style.

river houses have no numbers. They are designated by the foot of the street which they face. For instance, West's address is the Foot of Two Hundred and Fifth Street and North River. The majority of them have been in the same location for twenty-five or thirty years. A few moved down from the Inwood waterfront when the Department of Parks took that over. The oldest organization in the neighborhood is the Colonial Boat Club. It is the only one that still features rowboats.

The water along this shore is calm. Tall poles stuck in the mud serve for mooring masts. Their very irregularity forms a Japanesey pattern that makes a gorgeous picture.

Theodore Roberts, the champion outboardster, runs things at West's. He was busy tarring the roof the morning we called.

"This outboard stuff isn't a new game." He climbed down to talk. "They were at it in 1904. But it's only been popular in the last four or five years."

Our conversation was interrupted by the crack of a rifle shot.

"What are they shooting?" we asked.

"Firing at rats," Mr. Roberts explained. "That's open-air sport up here."

The huntsman on West's boat club dock was Charles Van der Beck, a member. The rifle he used was old and beautifully carved on the stock and barrel.

"That's a museum piece you're firing with," I said.

"Guess so," said the boy. "My grandfather made the stock and his father made the barrel. I have a pistol that's one hundred and fifty years old."

The Van der Becks originally spelled their name Van der Beeck. Hendrick was Charles's grandfather. His initials are on the gun.

"Yep, I s'pose our family is an old one," Charles said. "They say it goes back to Dutch days when this island was New Amsterdam and this part, Nieuw Haarlem."

Farther down we met an old man crabbing. "I come up here every day," he said, "I've been crabbing off these rocks for many years. I like the quiet."

He was a Hungarian, from East Seventy-Third Street, New York's Little Hungary. The rocks he stood on were lashed by a swift current, quite different from the gentle cove where the little boats swung at anchor. His trap was a primitive one of wire netting, in the shape of a box. He stuck a piece of bait in it, tied it to a strong rope, and swung it out in the water as far as he could, holding fast to the rope as he did so.

"Doesn't the sewer make the crabs dangerous to eat?" I asked.

"It hurts fishing back there," the old man answered, nodding in the direction of Captain Windle's docks, "but it doesn't bother us down here."

The sewers are a blot on the waterfront. The shoreline, that covers the pipes, is coated with a thick slime. The backwash is fetid and the air heavy with sickening odors. The big sewer which empties directly below Captain Windle's basin, causes him a great deal of trouble. None of his boats can remain at anchor any length of time near it. A tiny worm which hatches in filth, attaches itself like a barnacle to the under surface of the boats. It gradually eats into the wood.

Another one of these sewers empties directly below Washington Bridge. Aside from the stench they bring, the decaying matter dumped into the river makes the water unhealthy.

"Fishing would be much better," an old-timer in a boathouse this side of Washington Bridge told us, "if the Hudson were free of sewers!"

The most picturesque spot that we struck on the upper Hudson was Jeffery's Hook Lighthouse. Small, red, squatty, and ancient, it stands beneath George Washington Bridge. "By the swiftest waters in the Hudson," said Captain Windle.

John Gundelsheimer was the keeper we were told. He lived in the old-fashioned gray, weather-beaten frame house called the Fort Washington Yacht Club, at the foot of One Hundred and Fifty-eighth Street and the Hudson. On stormy nights he has to get up and start the fog-horn going. They say he never misses a fog. The neighbors were sorry. The horn always sounds like a cow. It wakes them up.

Some say that the lighthouse got its name from Captain Richard Jeffery, who lived around the middle part of the eighteenth century and gained his title as commander of the privateer *Greyhound*. Though Reginald Pelham Bolton believes it is a corruption of Geoffroix.

Jeffery's Hook is directly opposite One Hundred and

Seventy-Seventh Street off the banks of Fort Washington Park. The Continental Army during the first years of the Revolution used Jeffery's Hook for the point of obstruction. The Hudson is very narrow in these waters.

It was pleasant to find at this part of our walk, the old footbridge suspended above the railroad tracks. Few of this type remain. The quaint bridge adds to the charm of the little park.

On this side of Washington Bridge, as you follow the drive up, stands an old mansard-roofed house owned by the Department of Parks. Like the Carman mansion on the Speedway, the lower portion is used for administration offices, and the upper is converted into apartments that are rented by the month.

Inwood was restricted on the waterfront. A high fence protected it from the New York Central tracks. Rip-rap edged the shore. Isn't that a lovely name? It means the stone breakwater wall.

The little neck of land beneath the bridge, however, has always been ideal. People can get to it. Great trees shade it. There are pleasant winding paths wandering down the hillside and a natural beach where, they told us, in summer children came for blocks around to swim.

But either side of this lovely strip is flanked by sewers. One empties directly below Captain Windle's shipyard and causes him a great deal of trouble.

The old house which used to show its rooftops above the viaduct at One Hundred and Fifty-Sixth Street and the river, belonged to James Audubon, the naturalist. He called it Minniesland, when he purchased it in 1842.

Here he carried on his studies of birds and did much of

his writing. It was also in the Audubon house that Samuel F. B. Morse, inventor of the telegraph, conducted some of his experiments.

As apartment buildings encroached upon Minniesland, a group of public-minded citizens banded together and paid for the cost of moving Audubon's house piece by piece to the park this side of Washington Bridge, above Jeffery's Hook. When the admirers of Audubon got the house there, the money they had collected gave out. Two years ago, all that remained of Minniesland Mansion was carted away by the Department of Parks.

Along about 1907, the city began encroaching upon the Hudson River waterfront land in the vicinity of Audubon's home.

The great naturalist's estate ran from One Hundred and Fifty-Fifth Street to One Hundred and Fifty-eighth Street and extended from Amsterdam Avenue to the river. The Audubon family kept it intact until 1864.

Here, during the lifetime of James Audubon, wild birds such as turkeys, ducks, geese, and a variety of songbirds, enjoyed a haven. Rolling meadows flanked the east end of the property, great trees shaded the west side. Washington Irving often visited Minniesland.

In later years, the Audubon house became a roadside inn. I recall it as a little girl. My memory of it was a large square drab wooden house topped off by a very homely mansard roof. They say that Jesse Benedict, who bought the place from Audubon's sons, put on this roof.

During Audubon's occupancy, a sloping terrace of vivid green grass stretched its length to the sandy shores of the Hudson. A clear brook ran through the grounds.

Today, a portion of the site is a mass of huge concrete buildings. Reginald Pelham Bolton lives at 638 West One Hundred and Fifty-Eighth Street on a section of the former Audubon property. His garden is protected by a piece of fence built by Audubon. Riverside Drive traffic rumbles above those who attempt to follow the old Audubon Lane. The viaduct overshadows the streets. The sandy beach where Audubon watched for river birds is now a dumping ground for the street-cleaning department.

A gusty wind fluttered a storm of trash in our wake as we hurried through the streets past the birdman's old estate. Barred docks of the street-cleaning department kept us from the riverfront. We were eager to return to it. But we were not to get back to the waterfront until One Hundred and Twenty-Fifth Street. Not only street cleaning, but coal-barge piers made shore-line walking impossible.

Twenty-Seven

Ships Old and New

FORT LEE FERRY
MATJE DAVIT'S FLY

SHIPS with stories! There are plenty of them along the banks of the Hudson if you go looking for adventure boats.

We came across a great many in our waterfront wanderings. The most spectacular of the lot was a rum runner in drydock at the yards of the Half Moon Yacht Club on One Hundred and Forty-Eighth Street and the Hudson River, just below Simpson's Boat Works.

The cruiser had been painted a dark gray. We caught sight of it before we came to the clubyard. It was long and lean and mean-looking, with a bow built for speed and decks tripped to the gunwales.

"That boat must have a history," I said. "Let's stop and ask questions."

There was a grim air about the Half Moon Club yards. Heavy pieces of iron and steel machinery surround the main building. Through the upper windows of the yellow-frame house, we could see a man with binoculars, peering up and down the river. When we crossed the yard, another man, standing near the window, caught sight of us and poked his head out to ask what we wanted.

"Can you tell us something about this boat?" we called to him.

"That's a rum runner," came back the reply. He did not invite us into the clubhouse.

"It looks as if it had seen service," I yelled against the wind, which was blowing a gale.

"It has," our friend shouted.

We moved closer to get a better view of the sinister craft.

"What's that for?" I shrieked, pointing to something like a pipe, the one thing left visible above decks.

"Machine-gun base," hollered back the man. Against his better judgment, he was being drawn into the conversation. Reluctantly, he joined us.

"They say this boat's the only rum runner that's never been captured," he said. "The Coast Guard admits they've never caught up with her since she went into action."

"Who built her?"

"The Navy. She belonged to Admiral Josephthal during the war. Her name was *Conejos*. Cost something like sixty thousand dollars. That baby can run!"

"Are her running days over?"

"Well, she's been in drydock for a while. A new fellow bought her, says he's goin' to make a houseboat out of her." The man laughed.

Ruth Steinway and I walked on. We turned back once to take a last look at the boat. Two other men had joined the one we were talking to. They were watching us.

I am sure that we have been the subject of many a winter fireside conversation in waterfront clubs and homes.

When we told the people we stopped to talk with that we were walking around Manhattan Island they were dumbfounded.

"How long has it taken you?" they demanded. And then asked questions about different localities. We carried news of one section to that of another. Few leave their own neighborhood and as for getting into the heart of the city—that is a journey not attempted by many! When they do come they speak of "going into town."

On the trips, we have met friends. One of them Hans, the old sailor, we discovered aboard the *Mopelia*, Count Felix von Luckner's picturesque schooner anchored at the foot of One Hundred and Fifty-Seventh Street and the Hudson River.

Mrs. Steinway had brought her children up to meet Hans a couple of years ago when Count von Luckner was here. I once did a story of Hans. He's a sailor who knows his ropes. And that is literally speaking. He understands the meaning of each rope on a sailing vessel—there are not many who do today. He is small and lean and wiry, with twinkling little eyes, grizzled whiskers, and a friendly smile.

"I'm good for another ten years," he told us. "But I won't be if they keep me in port many more months. I've been here so long now the dogs don't bark anymore when they see me. That's terrible!"

He usually wears gold earrings in the form of anchors. "Where are they?" I asked.

"Oh, in my duffle-bag. I h'an't got the heart to put them on."

The Count was over in Germany. "Maybe we'll all get our sailing orders to come back," Hans said hopefully, as we left.

The *Mopelia* formerly anchored off the docks at the foot of Seventy-Ninth Street,—a broad, spaciously built, seaworthy vessel.

The Count and his wife lived on the *Mopelia* while they were in this country. Several officers of the boat, Hans, and a little dachshund still make it their headquarters.

The *Mopelia* and two other schooners are the only old windjammers on the Hudson River. One is a former training ship, now anchored opposite One Hundred and Fifty-First Street, and the other is a sea scouts' vessel at the foot of Seventy-Ninth Street, but its masts have been removed!

Captain John Gully, skipper of the *Ke-toh*, a deep-sea fishing boat, ties up near the Fort Lee Ferry, Matje Davit's old fly. His vessel was formerly the *Calumet*, a steam yacht owned by James J. Farrell, the United States Steel man.

We stopped to visit with the Captain at the One Hundred and Twenty-Fifth Street docks, where his boat was tied up. He mourns the passing of square riggers.

Captain Gully had seven brothers, and, like himself, they were all harbor men. His two boys are also on the water.

"It's in our blood," he said with a far-away look in his blue eyes. "I carry pictures o' things I've seen at sea, round in me mind now." He paused. "The best of them is a memory of the *Young America*, the fastest sailing vessel afloat when I was a lad.

"I was on a pilot boat that was goin' out to bring her in one night. There was a good stiff breeze, and the moon was full. All of a sudden, across the sea, we sighted the *Young America*. She was a kinda silvery white in the moonlight—with all sails up, steerin' a steady course. I'll never forget her."

Twenty-Eight

The Columbia Yacht Club

CAMP THOMAS PAINE YACHT CLUB

THE Columbia Yacht Club at the foot of West Eighty-Sixth Street, is the most up-and-coming yacht organization on Manhattan Island. Though the New York Yacht Club at the foot of East Twenty-Sixth Street may be a trifle more Social Registerish, the Columbia, on the whole, draws about the same crowd. Its clubhouse is in active use, while that of the New York Yacht Club is more a point of departure and arrival, than a tarrying place.

It was a bright, crisp autumn day when we stepped from the filled-in ground above the Columbia Yacht Club property to the trim, grass-edged walk that leads to the private landing of the club-house. We weren't supposed to be there, but "No Admittance" signs had not stopped us yet, so we kept on going.

The Columbia Yacht Club was founded in 1867. Headquarters

were then at the foot of West Fifty-Seventh Street. In 1874 the club moved up to the foot of West Eighty-Sixth Street and the Hudson River, its present home.

At that time, everyone thought fashionable New York would follow Riverside Drive. Physically it was the most beautiful section of the city. For a time, the Drive did go Fifth Avenue.

Jim Fair, father of Mrs. Graham Fair Vanderbilt, erected a magnificent home in the West Seventies on Riverside. Amelia Bingham had a red house with white marble statues at Eighty-Third Street and the Drive. Bishop Henry Codman Potter, stepfather of Ambrose Clark, lived at Eighty-Ninth Street. Matthews, the soda-fountain man, had a house not far from the Bishop's; Charles Schwab erected a huge mansion on Seventy-Fourth and the Drive, and Mrs. Isaac Rice built that great big maroon and white brick mansion where Mrs. Leon Schinasi lives now, on the south side of Eighty-Ninth and the Drive.

Mrs. Rice founded the Anti-Noise Society of New York. She was one of the few people who practice what they preach. A feature of her residence was a huge cave, cut out of the rock at the rear of the house, where she could retreat to a noise-proof room. She spent most of her time in it. I wonder if it is still there?

In short, it was the smart district in which to live. And then, for some reason, Social Register New York shifted to the East Side. But, though Fifth and Park rank high socially, Riverside Drive is still the most attractive residential portion of Manhattan Island.

The Soldiers and Sailors Monument, which old Mr. James Dwyer of the Marble Mansion put up, had not been completed when I was little. The white marble shafts used in the building of it, lay lengthwise on the ground, like the ruins of a Grecian temple.

The rows of fine homes that ran the length of the Drive were detached, with landscaped grounds about them. The house that stands out in my memory, is that of Mr. Matthews. His residence held a peculiar fascination for me as a child. It was a rambling light brownstone mansion and it stood on the northeast corner of Eighty-Ninth Street and Riverside Drive.

Rumor swept round among the children of the neighborhood that Mr. Matthews had installed a private soda fountain in his own home. None of us knew him, although we longed to make his acquaintance.

I lived at 588 West End Avenue. Whenever my family missed me, they eventually located me in front of the Matthews house trying to learn further details about the soda fountain.

Among the early settlers of West Eighty-Ninth Street was Charles Starbuck, Commodore of the Columbia Yacht Club. His home was on Eighty-Ninth Street and West End Avenue in an English basement house with an elaborate black wrought iron and crystal-glass canopy over the entrance.

Mr. Starbuck's lifelong friend was a Mr. Chaffee who shared the Eighty-Ninth Street house with him. Mr. Chaffee died very suddenly. The night he died, Mr. Starbuck left the house. He never put a foot in it after that.

Some of the better types of old New York mansions, built when Riverside Drive was a fashionable section of the city, linger on.

From our waterfront point of vantage at the river's edge and One Hundred and Eighth Street, we could see the white cupolas of the Semple School, formerly owned by Schinasi, the tobacco king. Hundreds of debs of this and other days who have graduated from Mrs. Semple's Academy are familiar with the big wedding cake-like structure, that boasts plumbing washed in gold, Italian mosaics on the bathroom floors, and rooms done entirely in Circassian walnut.

In contrast to this marble palace above us, was the straggling Patchtown settlement at our feet.

The Columbia Yacht Club House is a charming little spot. The exterior looks like some pleasant summer seaside cottage of stained shingled wood with sloping roof and dormer windows.

A private footbridge connects it with Riverside Park. I often wonder if there isn't a great waiting list of members. It's such a nice place to go. When the weather is warm, bright canopies are stretched over tables along the shore, where one may sit and have light refreshments. The interior of the clubhouse is old-fashioned, but it's very pleasant. The walls are paneled in dark wood and there are some fine old prints of early sailing ships in the big front room.

Yachts have their uses. Brigadier-General Cornelius Vanderbilt steamed round from the New York Yacht Club anchorage at the foot of East Twenty-Sixth Street and the East River to the Hudson River and West Eighty-Sixth Street in his sea-going yacht, the *Winchester*, the evening that General Italo Balbo, the Italian aviator, was guest of honor at the Columbia Yacht Club. The distance across town from the Vanderbilt home at Fifty-First Street and Fifth Avenue to Eighty-Sixth Street and the Drive could have been covered in less than half an hour by motor. I don't know how long it took the General to sail about in his yacht, but I am sure he had a lot more fun out of the trip, even if he didn't make time.

Another novelty is ham and eggs that are enjoyed by Tom Lamont aboard the Lamont yacht each morning when the swift little cruiser conveys the financier from his Englewood residence on the Hudson past the Columbia Yacht Club to Wall Street.

A trifle less luxurious but equally famous is the large flat-bottomed side-wheeler that plies in the summer between New York and the Atlantic Highlands, and sometimes gets up the Hudson. It is called the *Mobjack*.

Fifty years ago the *Mobjack* was a swift greyhound in Chesapeake Bay waters. It trundled round-about Norfolk and Cape Charles, carrying on its decks the belles and beaux of the period. At that time a voyage on the *Mobjack* was considered one of the fashionable pastimes. Many Virginians now living in New York recall much talked of voyages on it.

As we skirted the front yard of the club, we saw two very magnificent yachts at anchor in the river.

"Who owns those boats?" we asked a man at work on the grounds.

"Atwater Kent owns one of them," he answered. "And I think it's a Mrs. Moran has the other." He looked at us with curious but friendly eyes.

"And where did you ladies come from?" he asked.

"We're walking around Manhattan Island," we explained.

"Some walk," he said. "Well, ye'll be seein' sights below here. There's Camp Paine ye're approachin'."

He nodded at a far-off group of straggling little buildings huddled along the waterfront.

The land between the club and Seventy-Ninth Street dock has been filled in recently. A jagged line of granite rocks formed the only shoreline up to a few years ago. A wide dirt road now leads directly from the foot of West Seventy-Ninth Street to the Columbia Yacht Club. This was the one that we took. The afternoon was cold and blustering. The few shanty-town shacks scattered along the riverfront swayed beneath the stiff west wind.

"Cold weather's starting early for you, isn't it?" we called to some men grouped around the little buildings.

"We're trying to keep it out with tar paper," one man called back, waving a flapping length of it.

This little settlement had nothing to do with the Camp Thomas Paine group farther down, though some of the men said they were World War veterans.

One of the boys we talked to had been a sailor. His cabin and those nearby had little porches, new wood boxes, windmills, and garden fences. The sailor, handy at carpentering, had put things in order. He liked to garden. Frost-bitten zinnias and hollyhocks filled the tiny space that he had marked off for a flower bed.

A former occupant of his house had been an Indian, also an ex-soldier, they said. He had a feeling for art. His outlet had been in murals on his roof and side walls. They were of airplanes, machine guns, and no-man's land.

While some of the men in this particular settlement were of the professional out-of-work type, the majority were a grade higher, who belonged rather to the unemployed skilled artisan class than the panhandlers.

By far the most systematically run settlement that we had

walked through, was Camp Thomas Paine, just below the West Seventy-Ninth Street docks.

These docks were formally used as anchorage for boats such as the *Mopelia*, and Inglis Uppercu's auxiliary schooner, *The Seven Seas*, as well as traveling show boats, coal barges, and sand scows.

A wide boarding barred the way, the afternoon we crossed the docks. They say they have been condemned.

A floating lunch barge was the only craft at anchor. We stopped for a cup of hot tea and a doughnut. It was rather a cheerful place, warm and cozy after the walk against the wind. A square counter with high stools grouped around it filled the center of the cabin. An old barge captain stood near the stove. Back of it rose a white marble column. Resting on the shaft was a bust of Marie Antoinette.

"That's a funny thing to find here," Mrs. Steinway said.

"Where did you get it?" I asked the barge captain.

He looked at it thoughtfully and gave an extra puff on his pipe before replying. "Came from some big house on Long Island, that a friend of mine used to own," he said. "The fellow lost everything but Marie Antoinette in the depression. I'm keeping her for him."

Twenty-Nine

Patchtown

PATCH-TOWN

"Now, boys, let's put a little style on this roof. Make it snappy!" A carpenter whose night quarters were the floor of the Bowery Mission was speaking. With three other men, he busied himself piecing together a Rube Goldberg shack on the shores of the Hudson.

We were interested onlookers. Our waterfront meanderings had taken us to the first of the pathetic Patchtown houses that cling to the banks of the North River.

There are many—five hundred, I should say. Seventy-five are occupied by Bonus Expeditionary Force veterans.

"Fellows with honorable discharges," Commander Clark of the B. E. F. announced emphatically. But this is only at Camp

Thomas Paine, in the district below Seventy-Ninth Street. Above
—well, that's another story.

From Dyckman Street down to Seventy-Ninth Street the
tiny one- and two-room huts snuggle against cliffs and beach.
The homeless people who have taken possession of these lonely
shacks or built them are not of the flop-house variety. The
majority are eager, energetic, and courageous human beings who
have suddenly found themselves without money or work.

They were making ready for the winter when we saw them.
The pitiful little lean-tos that sheltered the lot offered scant
protection against cold winds. Extra boarding was needed.

If they worked in groups the people who lived in them were
able to fix the walls for the winter by doubling their thickness.
They all had a plucky attitude, these Patchtown folks.

"My husband and I don't know the first thing about building a
house," one woman told us. "But there are two carpenters nearby,
and they said they'd put up a winter shack for us—that they had
no work to do and they might as well be busy at something."

The two men needed a third for the roofing, so they got
hold of the Bowery Mission fellow because he knew how to fit
a roof on.

The woman could cook. She and her husband had a couple of
dollars that they put into food. The three carpenters were given
meals, the old man walking up every morning from the Bowery
to get his before he started to work.

"If we don't help one another we won't get anywhere," the
carpenter said. They were going at that house hammer and
tongs when we left. All they needed was cement. The rest of

the building material they had fished out of the junk pile. It's surprising what you can make use of when you have to.

We went inside a great many of the homes. While a few were ragged and untidy, the majority showed evidence of good house-keeping and background.

A man whose patchwork cottage lies just below Grant's Tomb had rigged up an old steamer chair in his tiny landscaped garden. He cooked on an outdoor grill made of iron grating that rested on top of well-placed stones. Oil lamps furnished reading light. His voice was cultivated and his manner that of a gentle-man. Though his suit was worn, it was of well-chosen tweed. He must have been in his early forties.

"One must live, you know," he said. "I go into town every day for work, but it's difficult to find. I've been here since spring. The summer has been delightful, but I don't know about the winter."

The people who live in the big apartment house at 33 River-side Drive were interested in the gay little shanty town that sprang up like a multi-colored mushroom at Seventy-Fifth Street and the Hudson River in 1932.

From the windows of George Gershwin's former penthouse at Number 33, with the aid of a spy-glass, every detail of the strange village could be clearly seen, as the work began on the huts.

To begin with there was just a single small shack, shuffled to-gether like a house of cards. One by one other little huts timidly put in an appearance until the settlement assumed the aspects of a miniature village.

When it first appeared, gossip rocked Number 33 concerning the meaning of the settlement. The little overnight village that caused so much speculation as to the people who lived in it was an aftermath of the B. E. F. group. The men encamped there were members of the Bonus Expeditionary Forces that marched on Washington.

The B. E. F. campers are now seasoned veterans. This has been their second winter on the banks of the Hudson. "And, boy, haven't we learned how to beat them river winds!" said Commander Clark.

An unemployed architect in camp drew up plans for a general recreation hall. Three carpenters, also in the camp, built it. The interior wood was taken from the old Bank of United States at Seventy-Ninth Street and Broadway.

"They gave it to us for hauling it away," explained the Commander. It is nicely paneled mahogany.

The fireplace, which reached to the roof, was made of rocks picked up from the shore. The camp was a beehive of activity with everybody getting ready for cold weather when we called.

"We'll sure be snug this year," Clark said.

In 1932 there were three hundred men in the settlement at the foot of Seventy-Fifth Street and Riverside Drive. The reforestation camp took one hundred and twenty-five, and about one hundred more got work around town.

"You'd be safe in saying seventy-five are still here," said the Commander, a tall, lean, tanned, weather-beaten man. He knew who Thomas Paine was. "I have The Rights of Man on my bookshelf," he remarked.

Camp Thomas Paine, as well as the Patchtown shacks, are on city property. Part of it belongs to the Department of Docks and part to the Department of Parks.

"What do you do about these people living down here ?" I

asked a policeman in the Schuyler Lunch, at the foot of Seventy-Ninth Street and the North River.

"They gotta live. We let 'em alone," he answered laconically. "They're good citizens."

"Don't write about us," some of them begged. "The city'll drive us away. We'll be sent to the Municipal Lodging House. God, we'd rather go any place than there! We're not bums!"

They certainly are not. I suggest that either the city give them steady work in cleaning up the waterfront and making a park of the uncultivated land where they are now living or that the state put them to work on a cooperative farm, in which they might hold shares. These men and women are not of the type to be sent to the poorhouse. If they had lived just after the Civil War they would have gone West. Now, they are doing their pioneering along the Hudson River waterfront.

Thirty

Commodore Vanderbilt's Pride and Joy

FLAG-MAN'S HOUSE
N.Y. CENTRAL R.R.
145TH ST AND THE HUDSON

WE REACHED Twenty-First Street and the Hudson River on the third of November. The wind was blowing a gale. It had been heavy going along the West-Side shoreline. We scrambled over rocks, took puddles with a run, skip and jump, and collected brambles galore in our effort to stick to the river.

Time and again watchmen stopped us with, "Hey! Ye can't go through here!" But we went. Most of the men lent a sympathetic ear to our pleadings. "Well, if ye'll take it at yer own risk, go ahead," they said. "But don't blame me if ye get stuck."

Once the only way out for us was over a high fence. We dis-covered a ladder-like run of boards that could be climbed. Not knowing just what we would find on the other side, we took a chance—and found the third rail. For five blocks we dodged the box-enclosed rail that spelled death. Far above us rose Riverside Drive and towering apartment-houses. To our right were the churning waters of the Hudson, lashed by the wind; our path was narrow, bordered on the left by the New York Central tracks.

An aged watchman shouted to us, as we neared a milk depot, "Ye're all right, if ye keep yer skirts away from the rail!"

We did. From One Hundred and Twenty-Fifth Street down we were able to avoid the tracks. There is enough filled-in land in this section to permit a wide road and ground for Patchtown. At Seventy-Second Street we left the rugged shores of the Hudson.

"Well, I guess that's the last of our climbing," Ruth Stein-way said.

Once more the New York Central tracks faced us. But this time there was enough space to avoid the third rail without picking the way.

The old roundhouse below the Chatsworth Apartments, at Seventy-Second and the Drive, is an interesting spot, though little used today, I imagine. Steam-engines are a thing of the past on the New York Central tracks along the Hudson, now electri-fied from Harmon down. To me, there is something fascinating about railroad yards.

The loading and unloading of merchandise, everything from glassware to automobiles, the shunting back and forth of the huge cars, and the excitement and bustle of the men at work suggest a George Bellows drawing.

The pride and joy of old Commodore Vanderbilt's life was this particular portion of the New York Central in the days when the railroad station was in the thirties, near Twelfth Avenue. Little remains of the original setup, save perhaps the stationmasters' quaint, wooden houses. We saw one at about One Hundred and Forty-Second Street and the Hudson. There are several below Fifty-Ninth Street. They are not in use.

The greatest number of piers on the Hudson River waterfront belong to the New York Central Railroad Company. Their most important yards used to be in the neighborhood of West Thirtieth Street, but the building of this new viaduct, in whose shadow we walked, may change matters. The larger bulk of shipping may be shifted to St. John's Park.

Their stations include the freight yards that extend from Fifty-Ninth to Seventy-Second Streets along the waterfront, the Manhattanville terminal at One Hundred and Twenty-Ninth Street on the Hudson, and the Saint John's terminal at the end down on Varick and Laight Streets.

This is the celebrated property, once a churchhouse square for which the first Commodore Vanderbilt paid one million dollars cash. A single check for that amount, to be cashed and divided among the shareholders of St. John's Park, was signed by him when the sale was made.

An experimental strap-iron track, completed after five and a half years of effort by the Mohawk & Hudson Railroad Company in 1826 was the nucleus from which has been developed the railroad system known as "The New York Central Lines." The Mohawk & Hudson was the first railroad to be operated in the state of New York and one of the first to be established in America. In the century after regular trains were first run over the seventeen miles between Albany and Schenectady that pioneer venture has grown into the great transportation system it is today.

First in the sequence of events that led to the foundation of the New York Central Railroad was the belief of George W. Featherstonhaugh, of Duanesburg, New York, that a steam locomotive running on iron rails would be an improvement over any system of transportation in vogue in 1812. Although he was considered a rich man, with a reputation as an explorer, scientist, and author, and numbered among his friends the most distinguished men of his time, Featherstonhaugh for a long time could convert no one to his views. Common folk ridiculed his idea about railroads.

As no one else would take the initiative, Featherstonhaugh, joined by Stephen Van Rensselaer, the last patroon, applied to the New York Legislature for a charter for a railroad to be called "The Mohawk & Hudson Rail Road," to run between Albany and Schenectady. This was the first link in what afterward became the New York Central Railroad. The charter was granted April 17, 1826. Construction began in 1830.

The first train carrying passengers on the Mohawk & Hudson Rail Road, August 9, 1831, was drawn by the famous locomotive "DeWitt Clinton," built at the West Point foundry in New York City. In the seven years from 1832 to 1839 the Mohawk & Hudson earned $692,800, more than eight-tenths of which was from passenger traffic.

Meanwhile, a charter for a railroad between Schenectady and Buffalo, thus completing a through route between the Hudson and Lake Erie, had been sought in 1831, but refused by the Legislature. Vast sums, that is, vast for those days, had been expended in building the Erie Canal, and the Legislature did not propose to permit competition. Even in 1836 when, in response to urgent demands from the public, a railroad between Schenectady and Utica, seventy-seven miles, was authorized, it was permitted to carry only passengers and their personal baggage. By 1844 the Legislature could see no harm in allowing the railroad to carry freight in winter when the canal was frozen up. Not until 1847, however, was permission to carry freight throughout the entire year granted, and then only upon condition that the railroad should pay to the state the same toll per mile for freight carried as the canal would have earned for the same service, a restriction imposed upon all railroads within thirty miles of the Erie Canal, and enforced until 1851.

In spite of this, enthusiasm for railroads grew from day to day. A road between Rochester and Batavia, thirty-three miles, was opened in 1837; between Utica and Syracuse, fifty-three miles, in 1839; between Auburn and Rochester, seventy-six miles, in 1841; between Attica and Buffalo, thirty-eight miles, in 1842. In 1843 the final gaps were closed, completing a line between Albany and Buffalo, but it was not operated as a through line.

On the contrary, all these little railroads were operated under independent ownership. On July 10, 1843, a fast express service between Albany and Buffalo was instituted, enabling travelers for a fare of eleven dollars and fifty cents to ride "in the best cars" in the breath-taking time of twenty-five hours, a trip now made by the Empire State Express in five hours, thirty-five minutes. In

1848 the time was cut to twenty-two hours. In 1850 the rate was slashed to nine dollars and seventy-five cents.

Three years after the rate cut was made an event took place which marked a new era in railroad industry. Pursuant to authority granted by the Legislature ten little railroads between Albany and Buffalo were consolidated into a single corporation under the name of the New York Central Railroad. The new management assumed control August 1,1853. Erastus Corning, the first president of the consolidated roads, and John V. L. Pruyn were the masterminds of this merger.

One of the important factors in producing the results that followed consolidation was the advent of Commodore Cornelius Vanderbilt in the New York Central management a few years later. Commodore Vanderbilt was the first outstanding genius in the railroad world, and he still ranks among the very few great economic statesmen in railroad history. His prophetic eye foresaw the growth of a rich empire in the heart of New York State if only adequate transportation facilities were provided, and he devoted all his wonderful creative genius to providing these facilities.

When the Mohawk & Hudson was opened in 1831, steamboats had been operated between New York and Albany for twenty-four years. It was believed impossible to compete with these palatial steamers. Besides, the physical difficulties of constructing a railroad along the Hudson were numerous and great. The Harlem Railroad also opposed any attempt at railroad building along the river. The genesis of the Harlem Railroad dates back to 1832 when the line extended all the way from Prince Street to Fourteenth Street in New York City. Cars were drawn by horses.

Five years later it had reached the Harlem River. January 19, 1852, the road reached Chatham, one hundred and twenty-eight miles from New York and twenty-three miles from Albany.

The Harlem Railroad folk were sure they could handle all the business between New York and Albany without help. So while applications for charters to build a railroad along the Hudson were made from time to time, opposition was so strong that it was not until 1846 that the Legislature gave permission to build.

Prompt action followed. In July 1847, the Hudson River Railroad, as the new line was called, was opened to a point fifty-three miles from New York. On October 1, 1851, the road was in operation to East Albany. The creative genius of Commodore Vanderbilt saw that these two railroads ought to be united with the New York Central under one management if they were ever to amount to anything. The deal was affected by means of an agreement dated September 15, 1869.

The new railroad was christened the New York Central & Hudson River Railroad, November 1, 1871. A connecting link was completed, giving the Hudson River line a connection with the Harlem Railroad, thus making it possible to run passenger trains from the former line into the station at Forty-Second Street, New York City, switching passenger traffic from the old West-Side terminal and making the Hudson River tracks, a freight road from Spuyten Duyvil down, the course we followed.

Thirty-One

Digging Docks

WE DISCOVERED that our climbing days were not over.

At Fifty-Fourth Street and the North River, we struck a huge embankment of earth, stone breastworks, and mud.

"Let's not go round," Mrs. Steinway said; "it's much more

DOCK BUILDING W. 52ND ST

fun to keep to the waterfront. Perhaps we can get through."

"And where be ye ladies a-goin'?" asked Joe Reilly, the superintendent of works, as we plowed past his office.

"We're following the waterfront," we chorused.

"Ye'll have a hard time doin' it here. Ye're after goin' to a dead-end. Thim's barges off there. The Shamrock Towin' Co."

A bright emerald barge, the *St. Patrick* of New York, loomed up in front.

"Very well; we'll turn off here." We skirted a mud puddle. "What's happened to this land?"

"Docks," said Mr. Reilly, shifting his tobacco. "The city's buildin' them. They've been at it day and night now for two years. Got one more to go."

Outside of the Panama Canal, I've never seen anything quite so spectacular in construction. The size of the work, the steam shovels, great walls of cement, and mountains of rocks, make the dock-digging grounds a powerful picture. I should like to see it after dark when the huge searchlights are playing on it.

Mr. Reilly squired us back to the road. "Good luck to ye," he called.

The first dock in New York was built in 1648. It was a flimsy little wooden wharf run up on the East River. "For the convenience of the merchants and citizens," according to an old record. It served the people of New Amsterdam until a much more capacious landing known as the Bridge was erected ten years later at the foot of Moore Street. Then it was that the local government constructed a pier and proceeded to collect wharfage charges, a custom practiced to this day.

In 1676, the Great Dock was finished when the Bridge and a new pier formed a semicircle in front of the Staats Haus.

From 1686 to 1730, every person in New York owning water-front property had the right to erect a private dock. This is the way that Peck's Slip got its name, and Walton's Wharf happened to be called after that illustrious family.

Thomas Rush, one-time surveyor of the Port of New York,

says that it was not until 1798 that an attempt was made to give regularity to the bulkhead line and to plan streets for the wharves. To do this the intervention of the United States Government was necessary.

Federal aid, however, was seldom forthcoming. The first help that New York had from Washington was in 1851 when the government began deepening the waters of Hell Gate.

The Department of Docks was established in 1870. Three times as many trunk lines come to New York, as to any other city on the Atlantic Coast.

Between Seventy-Second and Fifty-Ninth Streets, there is a solid row of docks that handle nothing but freight car barges. The walking through this district is over rough cobblestone streets, beneath the new viaduct that now extends to Seventy-Second Street and Riverside Drive.

The wind was blowing a gale the afternoon Mrs. Steinway and I passed by these railroad docks. Our coats flapped against our ankles, our hair hung in straggling lengths and we had difficulty in keeping our hats on. We shivered while we watched the cars being brought up on barges, shunted off onto New York Central Railroad sidings, and unloaded. The railroad maintains six docks.

The greater part of the freight was automobiles. Bright, shining new motors were being handled with gloves, to keep the lacquered bodies from being scratched. The streets in this section of town are strangely deserted. Our highway—Thirteenth Avenue—marked the border-line of Hell's Kitchen, that section of New York famed in police annals of the past.

Great, red-brown gas tanks cast their shadow over the freight yards. Hungry-looking cats slink beneath refuse and there is always a wind whistling through the empty warehouses and factories that loom up on side-streets. These same buildings, they say, once harbored the Hell Kitchen Gangs. The devious alleys, dark passageways, and narrow courts offered easy getaways for the boys.

Occasionally along a wharf, you will find in this section— even as in any other New York river-front neighborhood—old men fishing. They belong, as do the ancient anglers of the Seine, to a vast club of fishermen. The only requisites necessary for joining are a rod and line or a plain length of twine to which has been attached a bent pin for a hook and a tiny brass bell that tinkles when a fish bites. The bells seldom ring. But that doesn't worry the old men. They like to sit and watch the boats go up and down the river. Fishing gives them an excuse.

The chief haul in Hudson waters is Tomcods. They're not very good to eat. Sometimes there is a run of Lafayettes and at rare intervals—rock bass and bluefish. Oil from ships, sewers, and chemicals kill the fish.

Another waterfront custom that intrigued us, was the building of little bonfires to keep warm. We felt like starting one ourselves. The working men had small braziers that they stuffed with odd bits of wood, to which they set a match. The cheerful red glow from the tiny blazes added to the color of the drab viaduct and gas-tank-shaded street, the cold afternoon we followed the river as far as Fifty-Ninth Street.

On our next walk, the day was so clear that we could see every house on the cliffs of the Jersey Shore. Great white clouds scuttled across the blue sky and tiny white-caps dotted the deep green-blue waters of the Hudson.

"Did you ever see anything so gorgeous ?" Ruth Steinway exclaimed. "I've never seen so much color."

The red of the piers, the black of the smoke-stacks on the big ocean liners, and the rainbow-hued barges helped bring life into the picture.

The New York State Barge Canal Terminal faces DeWitt Clinton Park at West Fifty-Fourth Street and Thirteenth Avenue. These barges are in active use. They are freshly painted. Their little storm houses are in good condition and their holds well-filled with cargoes of sand or gravel. It was difficult to reach the barges from the shore, because of the tremendous work in dock digging that had torn up half of DeWitt Clinton Park, obliterated Thirteenth Avenue, and thrown breastworks of mud in front of the wharf.

This barge terminal and the one that we saw at the beginning of our walk—the Coenties Slip Terminal—are the only two on Manhattan Island. There is another big barge port at Edgewater, New Jersey, near the Fort Lee Ferry. The route that practically all of the barges follow is up the Hudson to Albany, through the Champlain Canal to Lake Champlain, and on up into Canada. The sand barges are towed back and forth between Long Island and New York.

Thirty-Two

Pioneering With Ships

BACK of every big ship company there is a romantic story, and a cross-section of New York waterfront history.

The huge ocean greyhounds with their triple smokestacks, massive engines and Gargantuan proportions that we passed on the North River waterfront have been made possible because of the courage, sense of adventure, and will-power of the men who have built and manned the ships that have gone before. When the founders of these great transatlantic lines were considering their plans, America was in the making.

The shipbuilding plans of Thomas Clyde were underway for years before they could be brought into action. His combination steam and sailing vessel, *John S. McKim*, was commissioned for service in 1844. Her mechanical installation was under the personal supervision of Mr. Clyde and John Ericsson. The *John S. McKim* was the first screw-propelled steamer designed and built

in the United States for commercial purposes. Her new driving mechanism put her immediately at the forefront of American ships, since she had greater speed and stability, with more dependability and less vibration, than the side-wheel steamers which until then had ruled the waters.

The United States Government pressed the steamer *John S. McKim* into service for the Mexican War in 1846, using her as a transport to convey Colonel Jefferson Davis and his regiment of Mississippi Volunteers to the Mexican war front.

American shipping grew rapidly during the few years following the discovery of gold in California. Many a proud ship loaded with adventurers and cargo took her long course around Cape Horn to the new El Dorado. Other ships were needed to handle the growing commerce in our coastal waters and to foreign ports.

During the Civil War at least twelve ships flew the Clyde house flag, and the names of nearly all of them are inscribed in the imperishable annals of service of the Federal Government. One ship, the *Liberty*, operating on a line between New York and Washington, was sunk in the Potomac by Confederate gunfire, and the line was discontinued until 1868.

Upon the collapse of the Southern Confederacy, Jefferson Davis was captured, and in 1865 was placed as a prisoner of war aboard the Clyde steamer *Rebecca Clyde* and transported to Fort Monroe where he was imprisoned.

The East and the West were united by rail in 1869.

The United States Government in 1870 established what was to become one of the greatest safeguards to shipping that could be imagined. It was the Weather Bureau whose functions then were virtually the same as to-day. In that day, however, weather reports and predictions were designed solely for the benefit of shipping and it was not until several years later that the service was extended to the field of agriculture.

To avoid the long trip around Cape Horn through the poorly charted Straits of Magellan, a new route was devised, and in 1876 the Clyde interests organized the Panama Transit Steamship Company to furnish cheap and quick transportation of passengers and freight between the Atlantic Coast and San Francisco and other Pacific ports.

Passengers and cargo were taken aboard at New York and were transferred to the Panama Railroad at Colon. They were then moved across the Isthmus by rail and again took ship at Panama City for the Pacific Coast ports. To operate in the Pacific end of this route the *South Carolina* was sent around the Horn, making the tempestuous journey in forty-six days, then considered a remarkable feat.

Thomas A. Edison invented the phonograph and the first elevated railroad was operated in New York City over the Sixth Avenue Line during 1878. Keeping step with progress, the Clyde Line converted the side-wheel steamers *Georgia*, *South Carolina* and *Morro Castle* to screw-propeller driven ships.

The financial condition of the country was now a little more stable. The population of the United States in 1880 was about fifty million. Garfield was elected. In this same year, a new Clyde steamer, the *Carib*, was put in service. She was later sunk early in the World War in European waters, while under charter to foreign shippers.

The Clyde Line's first *Cherokee* was completed in 1886. She and a sister ship, the *Seminole*, first of her name in the Line, were of iron, 264 feet long, of 1966 registered tonnage, and were constructed at Philadelphia.

Especially designed for service between New York and Jacksonville, they carried 166 passengers, with 49 members in their respective crews. These were the first Clyde Line steamers to have their passenger quarters in houses above decks instead of between decks. The first *Algonquin* and *Iroquois*, almost identical in design with the first *Cherokee* and *Seminole*, quickly followed them into service. Again, an interesting comparison may be made between the sizes and descriptions of these early ships, with their new namesakes in service to-day.

William McKinley was elected president in 1896, defeating William Jennings Bryan. Gold was discovered in the Klondike and the Spanish-American War was declared in 1898. Three Clyde liners, the *Cherokee*, *Comanche* and *Iroquois*, served the Government through that brief conflict. The *Comanche* was a new steamer, built in November, 1895, carrying 278 passengers. She was 320 feet 10 inches long, of 3202 tons register, and in 1901 was lengthened to 369 feet 4 inches, increasing her tonnage to 3856. The *Comanche* had the first quadruple-expansion engine.

Equally well associated with the history of New York's waterfront was the Cunard Line. Philip Hone speaks of Mr. Cunard of Halifax in 1840, when the famous clipper ship *Great Western* docked in New York, making it in eighteen days from Bristol, with Fanny Ellsler as well as the illustrious ship owner on board.

The *Hibernia* inaugurated the New York service of the Cunard Line in 1847. New York showed its appreciation of the importance of the Cunard Line, by holding a reception in the

Exchange for Captain Ryrie, skipper of the ship, to introduce him to the leading business men and merchants.

The present-day Cunard Piers run from Fifteenth to Little West Twelfth Streets. The *Mauretania*, *Berengaria* and *Aquitania* are their prize ships. Though the *Mauretania* is the speediest, the *Aquitania* is my favorite English ship.

The captains of all three, however, are interesting men. The skipper I knew the best was Captain Spencer McNeil of the *Mauretania*, who has recently been retired.

When the lobster fishermen were taking in their lobster pots off Ambrose Light, Captain McNeil would always get a few lobsters, if his ship happened to be near. With the proper fixings, the lobsters were prepared for the Captain's friends, when he got into port. The long cement floor dock of Pier 56 has led the way to many a nice dinner on the *Mauretania*.

The head of the Cunard Line to-day is Sir Ashley Sparkes. From his penthouse on top of the Cunard Building at 25 Broadway, he can sight his ships coming into port.

Not to be forgotten in North River waterfront lore, is the French Line. On February 24, 1855, under the leadership of two brothers, Emile and Isaac Pereire, a French navigation company was formed by the name of Compagnie Generale Maritime, its activities being chiefly devoted to fishing, equipping sailing vessels for fishing on the Banks of Newfoundland, and to several coastal services of Belgium, France, Spain, Portugal and Algeria.

Six years later, on August 25, 1861, this company, having received from the French Government contracts for the operation of a postal service to the West Indies, Mexico and the United States, changed its name to that of Compagnie Generale

Transatlantique, better known on this side of the Atlantique as the French Line. The first steamer to sail under its flag (a white flag with a red ball in the upper left-hand corner, and the name CIEGLE TRANSATLANTIQUE in red letters across the flag) was the *Louisiana*, and she made her first trip from Saint Nazaire to Vera Cruz (Mexico) in April, 1862. She was an iron screw steamer of 1780 tons gross, and one of a pair, the other vessel, a duplicate, being the *Floride*, built the same year at Greenock (Scotland) by Caird & Company.

The Cie Gle Transatlantique transferred its home port about this time from St. Nazaire to Le Havre.

From the start, an important building program was planned, and on June 15, 1864, the *Washington*, built at Greenock, was leaving Havre on her maiden trip bound for New York, which port she reached June twenty-ninth after having met adverse winds, rough seas and frequent fogs, fourteen days after her departure from her home port. Captain Duchesne was in charge of the *Washington*, and had a crew of fifty sailors, fifty stokers and mechanics, fifty stewards for the care of the passengers. Louis Bebian was the agent in New York, and his offices were at 6 Bowling Green where now stands the Custom House.

The following August, her sister ship, the *Lafayette*, made her maiden trip from Havre to New York. Each ship had about the same dimensions, both being fitted with side-lever engines, and were paddle-wheel driven iron ships. The captain of the *Lafayette* was de Bocade. The company's agent was then G. McKenzie. Another *Lafayette* was built in 1915, and this ship was a few years ago transferred to the Havre-Mexico service, and renamed *Meanque*, when the company built the new cabin liner, which

entered the Havre-New York service in May, 1930, and christened it *Lafayette*, after the French General who had offered his
services to the American Revolutionary Army.

The *Ville de Paris*, built in 1866, and the *Pereire*, completed in
1864, were fitted with one funnel and three masts. On her trial
trip the *Pereire* made 15.36 knots. The *Ville de Paris* made her trial
run on May 12, 1866, and achieved almost identical results.

As older vessels were withdrawn, newer and faster steamers
were built. In 1883, the popular *Normandie*; in 1886, *La Champagne*, *La Gasgogne*, *La Bretagne* and *La Bourgogne*. In 1891, the
fast twin-screw steamer *La Touraine*, with a speed of nineteen
knots, broke the record at that time. In 1914, *La Touraine* made
a few trips from Havre to Montreal (May 16th, 30th and June
13th). In 1900, *La Lorraine* and *La Savoie* entered the Havre-New
York service. The latter was still a popular ship when, in 1927,
after twenty-five years of service, the company sold it. In 1906
La Provence was launched. This boat, which was used during the
World War as a hospital and transport ship, was sunk in the
Mediterranean by a submarine. All these boats were named after
different provinces of France.

In June, 1921, the *Paris* made her maiden trip to New York.
She is my favorite of all. For many years, Captain Rene Puegnet,
was the Captain. He's a versatile man who not only sails a ship,
but plays the violin, paints, and speaks Sanskrit. Just now he is in
France superintending the construction of the *Normandie*, which
is to be the new flag-ship of the French Line. Captain Puegnet
will be the skipper.

In 1927, on June twenty-second, the flag-ship of the French
Line, the *He de France*, left Havre for New York, with every

modern apparatus and machinery, and the most up-to-date interior decoration and lighting system that could be found on any vessel afloat. On the eighteenth of August, 1928, the first ship-to-shore service was inaugurated when, from the stern of the *He de France*, there was catapulted an amphibian plane when the boat was some three hundred miles from New York, where it alighted near Quarantine Station four hours later, and delivered the air-mail, a saving of fifteen hours. The mail destined for Chicago reached that city about the same time that the *He de France* was docking at Pier 57 on the North River.

Uninteresting sheds, these piers are to look at, but those who walk them touch far corners of the world.

Thirty-Three

There's Always A Boat Sailing

THE OLD WOODEN HOUSE
AT 632 W. 52ND ST.

LONG lines of seamen curved out into West Street as we swung past the French Line piers. The *Paris* was docking. Taxicabs rattled up to the entrance of Pier 57. Excited crowds gathered in front of the elevators. Street vendors selling souvenirs, flowers, and magazines pushed their way through the throngs.

The fashionably dressed people looked strangely out of place on West Street. Not so the seamen, in their blue denim jeans, wool caps pulled well down over their ears, and heavy shoes that clop-clopped like sabots over the cobblestones. They belonged to the waterfront.

The dock workers are hired only when the ships arrive and depart. There is a Dutch look to their wide pantaloons and the swinging, lumbering gait they have. Today, we were told the majority of these men were Americans. Before the World War, seventy percent were Scandinavian born.

The North River waterfront from Fifty-Seventh Street down to the Battery is bounded by huge piers from which ships sail to practically every part of the world; the Swedish lines, then the Italian, next the Hamburg American, the United States Lines, which the Roosevelt family controls. First come the coastwise boats, Panama Pacific, the French Line, the Cunard, the North German Lloyd, the United Fruit, and a dozen and one smaller companies whose boats go to New England or the Southern States.

"You will be in the doldrums from Twenty-Third Street to Fourteenth," someone told us, when we headed down Twelfth Avenue, in the final lap days of our Hudson River walk.

Perhaps, our friend didn't have a feel for the sea and boats and far countries. To us, the flat, drab steel-enclosed piers spelled adventure, romance, and other lands. The great steamship companies of the world dock their liners at these huge cement blocks that jut out into the North River.

Pier 57 is famous as the New York berth of the *He de France*, the *Paris*, and other French boats. Pier 54 spells *Berengaria, Aquitania, Mauretania*, while Pier 59 is the dock at which the *Majestic, Britannic*, and *Olympic* tie up when they are in port.

The day that we walked up the piers was a windy, blustering,

November morning. Great trucks rumbled past us. The new viaduct for non-commercial vehicles cast its shadow across our path, which lay over bumpy pavements, and yet we liked it. We liked to watch the blue-smocked seamen. Their clothes had been worn long enough to take on the shapes of their huge bodies.

We liked the little shops that flanked the east side of the street. Strange places that catered with naive appeal to the simple tastes of the sailors. Cheap souvenirs, soaps, perfumes, and framed photographs of pretty girls, jumbled in with regulation seamen's caps, shirts, middies, and jackets, filled the windows. A few of the tiny stores had French or Spanish names, showing that the inlanders of the section which includes old French and Spanish settlements, had crept over to the waterfront.

And above all we liked that square honest feel that we found around the entire waterfront, a look that goes with the people who follow the sea. Even the poorest of sailors had it, a straight way of looking you in the eyes.

There are several charitable institutions for sailors along the West Side waterfront.

The first of the group is the New York Port Society at 168 Eleventh Avenue. Mrs. Steinway and I were attracted to it, because of the quaint, old-fashioned exterior. Its tan brick front, respectable dark-wooded trimmings, and anchor over the door lured us into it. We were curious. The chapel is on the first floor.

A sailor directed us up the narrow flight of stairs that led to the main hall. Dr. A. Lincoln Moore guides the destinies of the New York Port Society. His offices open off the hall where the seamen sit. There were not many sailors in the room the morning we called.

"Because there are not many ships in port," explained Doctor Moore. He is a pleasant-faced but strong-minded clergyman, determined in voice and ways.

The history of the New York Port Society is an interesting one. It was founded on a Sunday morning in May, 1818, because a seaman, whose identity could not be learned, had shinnied up a steeple to prevent a church from burning. The fire started in the spire, the unknown sailor put it out.

We lunched at the Seamen's Institute farther down on Eleventh Avenue and Twentieth Street. The cafeteria is run for the benefit of the sailors and officers in port. Like the busman on his proverbial holiday, we caught the sailors eating beans, a dish that we also ordered with pork. It was not expensive and proved well-seasoned and cooked.

The Seamen's Institute is a marine branch of the Y. M. C. A. The new building which they occupy was completed in 1930 at the cost of several million dollars. There is a swimming pool, and also a gymnasium which can be converted into a dance hall, as it is every Saturday night, recreation-room, dormitories, and a library.

The cost of a bed is forty cents a night. If the men have no money, they are sent down to the old Institute headquarters on Jane and West Streets. Eight thousand men a week pass through the new institution. Those we saw were chiefly young boys. They get their mail, leave their duffle bags, and spend their shore leave at the Institute.

Though primarily planned for American sailors, foreign seamen in port may also use the Institute. The only pass required is their papers showing what boat they have been or are on.

Along with the youngsters, the Institute, like all sailors' shelters, has accumulated its share of characters, old seamen who have put into port for good.

Though not open to the public, I am sure that if you ask at the desk in the main lobby the clerk will be glad to send a guide with you to show you through the building. George F. Robertson is the executive secretary in charge. When Mrs. Steinway and I called, he was busy working out an international soccer match with the athletic instructor of the *Bremen*. The difficulty lay in hitting boats that were in port at the same time. The *Rex*, the flag-ship of the Italian Line, had to jibe with the *Bremen*. The final contest lay between the crews of these two ships.

The Seamen's work of the New York City Y. M. C. A. was first organized as the Merchant Seamen's Branch on December 15, 1920, in a three-story building, which was believed to be wholly adequate to meet the needs for at least five years. It was equipped with dormitories for sixty men, a cafeteria that would serve about one hundred men a day, and a social room or lounge that would afford one hundred or two hundred men a place in which to meet their friends, write letters and enjoy a simple program of activities which was arranged. From the first day, the lounge was crowded to the doors. Fame of the place spread along the waterfront until it was soon enjoying an average daily attendance of twelve hundred.

Men were nightly refused hospitality because of lack of sleeping quarters, and hundreds were turned away daily because the building was too crowded for comfort. The sailors literally pushed out the walls, and forced the Y. M. C. A. to look about for a larger building in which to "carry-on."

Seamen's House, a new million-dollar building for the use of the men and boys of the merchant marine, the Seamen's Christian Association, the American Seamen's Friend Society, and the Toe H Ships Boys' Club, was dedicated on Wednesday evening, November 4, 1931, and formally opened on the following Friday evening by the New York City Y. M. C. A. These organizations dealing with seamen have merged their local work for sailors, and as a result, a new building has been erected at the corner of West Twentieth Street and Eleventh Avenue to house the many activities for the men and boys from the ships.

Seamen's House is eight stories in height. The building is done in the modern style of architecture, of brick construction with stone and terra cotta trimmings. It is, without doubt, the finest building in the world to be devoted to the interests of the crews of the passenger and freight ships of the seven seas.

The features include a big lobby, reading- and lounging rooms, as well as the game rooms, gymnasium, swimming pool, chapel, social and club rooms, cafeteria, two hundred and twenty-five sleeping rooms, and an open dormitory which I have touched upon. In addition to the quarters for men, there is a well-equipped boys' department for the use of the cabin boys and bell boys who work on the big liners. There is also provision made for looking after the activities of women who are employed as stewardesses on the steamers, this being the first building of the sort that has included these women in its work.

We put our coats in a room reserved for stewardesses when we went down to lunch.

The great need for a modern building of this sort is quickly seen when it is realized that on any day in the year, there are approximately twenty-five thousand employed seamen in the city. These men make up the crews of the ten thousand or more merchant ships that drop anchor in New York Harbor each year. The men come from the ships of all nations, and Seamen's House should prove to be an even greater center for them than the old quarters of the Merchant Seamen's Y. M. C. A. has been in the past.

Should the new building be too small in future years the foundation and steel construction will permit the erection of three additional stories with about two hundred more sleeping rooms.

Seamen's House helps men to find employment. Thousands of placements are made each year and along with these go a large amount of vocational counseling. Among other essential services to seamen are facilities for checking baggage, mail service, and banking facilities.

Thirty-Four

❧

Old and New on the West Front

LIVE POULTRY MARKET

DURING Thanksgiving week, we saw our fill of turkeys, guinea hens, and pheasants, as well as the old gray goose. They were strung up in river-front markets to tempt holiday marketers.

On this particular jaunt, we got as far as St. John's Park. It is a park in name only, however. In 1867, Commodore Cornelius Vanderbilt signed the memorable check for one million dollars, in payment for the little square on the Hudson River front, bounded by Varick and Laight Streets. Before the year was over, the great trees that had shaded it were chopped down, surrounding houses had disappeared, and rising as a phoenix out of the debris was the gaunt and barnlike structure built by the Commodore for a freight terminal to his Hudson River railroad.

To this day the terminal is spoken of as St. John's Park, though the ancient green square and quaint church, for which it is named, has long since vanished. The railroad is responsible for the rapidly changing character of a neighborhood that has been in turn fashionable, then picturesque, and now drab. The first phase ended with the building of the freight terminal, and the second phase vanished with the construction of the viaduct that was being hammered into being when we arrived on the scene.

Already the section through which Spanish sailors had tramped less than six months before, the little cafes in which they played banco and the old red-brick houses where they boarded, had sunken into oblivion.

Also preparing for a shifting of scenery, when we explored the district, was a miniature Patchtown Camp at Little West Twelfth Street and Death Avenue. The rapidly growing freight viaduct overshadowed it. The menagerie assortment of human beings that made their homes in the grubby packing boxes on the vacant lot, were pawing around for new quarters.

"Yes," said Detective Frank Campbell, of the Charles Street Police Station, "this neighborhood ain't what it used to be."

He pulled his black derby hat down to shade his eyes, leaned back in his swivel chair, and strummed on the top of his golden oak desk.

With hesitating questions, we faced the big-time detective of the Sixth Precinct.

"No more heavy stuff," continued Campbell in his husky bass. "The Hudson Dusters have dusted out. The viaduct's driven away the Chili boys, and art ain't spelled with a capital A in the Village these days. All we get now is an odd stick-up or automobile robbery. But none of it's new to write home about. Even Jimmie Walker's gone."

We wandered a bit off the beaten path to look at the erstwhile home of Mr. Walker at Number Six Saint Luke's Place.

A "For Sale and Rent" sign loomed up above the black wrought-iron lamps that marked the old-fashioned red-brick house as the residence of New York's one-time mayor. As this book went to press, the Walker house was sold.

Plain white scrim curtains veiled the dusty windows when we saw it. The small iron gate that separated the walk from the areaway swung aimlessly on its hinges and there was a deserted atmosphere about the tightly closed vestibule.

It's a far cry from this simple house where Jimmie once lived to his present home in France. The neighborhood people ask if he is homesick, among them Mrs. Steinway's laundress, Quinny, who remembers Jimmie Walker when he was a little boy. Katherine Quinn was eight years older than he, and a staunch admirer of his, as were all of the kids in Greenwich Village.

The sedate row on the north side of St. Luke's Square playgrounds housed not only Jimmie Walker but Starr Faithfull, the beautiful girl whose body was washed up on Long Beach a few years ago.

"And sure, the boys should have let that case die," said Detective Campbell. "It was nothing but suicide. Why did they have to dig up old bones?"

Starr Faithfull, and James J. Walker, each in their way, have brought fame to the quiet little square.

The square once had a white picket fence to encircle the graves that lay encompassed in it. And about which, Quinny said, the children used to play.

"Every day after sun-down," she told us, "we kids would hang on the fence outside the graveyard and yell 'Deadhead and bloody bones!' and then run for our lives."

Brick houses such as trim the north side of St. Luke's Place, linger wistfully on waterfront streets in Greenwich Village. Many have nicely carved doorways. A number are brightened by lattice-paned dormer windows and all are trimmed with slender black wrought-iron gratings that wind their balustrade way up the steps.

Teddy Roxbury, "The Duke" to his political friends in the Village, lived in just such a house at 149 Charles Street, until the viaduct drove him away. Mrs. Steinway and I passed Number 149 when we called on Detective Campbell. Though not in the direct path of the viaduct, it was vacant. When he was a little boy, Teddy Roxbury played on Charles Lane, locally known as Pig Alley. An old woman who tended pigs lived there. Her house opened on the Alley.

Ted Roxbury is Irish, as was the entire neighborhood at one time. With the coming of the Morgan Steamship Line, the section took on a Spanish and Portuguese flavor.

"The viaduct's scattered these sailors to the four winds," Detective Campbell said, "but if ye're lookin' for any, like as not you'll find them in the Spanish quarter down around Roosevelt and Cherry Streets."

There's character to this St. John's Park and Greenwich Village district that we explored, in spite of the dull drabness of vacant houses, empty streets, and deserted loft buildings.

Even in transition, the great viaduct with its orange and black steel girders, the falling sparks of the riveter's drill, and the shouts of the workmen, weaves a powerful picture, rich in modernistic angles.

It is strangely in contrast to the old dwellings, huge markets, and empty docks.

Few of the old waterfront hotels linger on West Street, a river's edge highway that once abounded in them.

Among those which we did discover, that had survived were the Christopher Hotel at Christopher and West Streets and the Keller-Abingdon House at 250 Barrow Street on the northeast corner of West Street.

The former is a tan building of mid-Victorian architecture. It was called in its heyday the Palace, and known to every waterfront visitor as well as many money-spending inlanders. The bar made it famous.

The gray winter morning that we climbed to the office on the second floor, we found scant traces of early style. The only evidence of better days was in the huge, old-fashioned mirror at the far end of the lobby.

"This used to be the sitting room," explained a clerk, "but stick-ups got pretty bad, so we moved the office here, where they couldn't reach us so easily."

The telephone was concealed in a large upper drawer of the old yellow oak roll-top desk.

"Why do you keep it there?" asked Mrs. Steinway.

"So strangers won't ring up numbers on us. We had eighty-five dollars extra to pay in long-distance calls last month."

Living is cheap at the Christopher Hotel. A large double front room with a bath is five dollars a week. We looked at one, a cheerful spot with plenty of light and air.

"We have some steadies," said the clerk. "Richard Mahoney, the engineer, he's a very big man, has been with us seventeen years."

But for the most part, the seafaring, money-spending trade has been replaced by truckmen who sleep during the day and drive all night. They work for various transportation lines that move freight by motor from the New England States. Some come from Pennsylvania and a few from New York State. They carry anything from shoes to celery. The trucking offices are a few blocks down from the two hotels we visited.

This trucking business is a new touch to the waterfront. It is running neck and neck with the huge railroad spurs that fight for trade from the very markets and commission houses that line the waterfront streets. The rumble of the trucks in a steady march along West Street drowns out the rattle of freight cars on Death Avenue. It is a fight to the finish. Just now the neighborhood people are betting on the trucks, particularly for short runs.

In one night, produce can be delivered to Providence and Boston, by truck, with no shifting of cargo at the starting or finishing line. No railroad can beat that.

More than half the rooms in the Keller-Abingdon House are leased by trucking firms for their employees.

"It's truckmen here, and not sailors," Oscar Goldberger,

proprietor of the hotel, said. "Shipping's dead. The trucking business is a going concern." The truckmen eat in the little coffee-pot
lunch-rooms along West Street.

COWBOY OF DEATH AVENUE

We stopped in the Great Western Coffee Pot at 264 Vestry
Street to warm our toes and pick up local news.

The place was full of great, heavy-chested, muscular-bodied
men eating turkey dinners at fifty cents a plate. They had a
simple way of carrying their implements of trade. One had an ice
pick strung around his neck, another tucked a monkey wrench
in his boot, and a third had an ax in his coat pocket.

Morris, the proprietor, kept a lively eye on his customers and
had a come-back that would do credit to an Al Jolson or Irving
Berlin. From Christopher to Laight Street, nondescript shops,
small, fly-specked pool-rooms, an occasional dormer-windowed
Colonial house, and a scattering of small hotels, fringe the waterfront. Beyond that—the Washington Market district begins.

Thirty-Five

⤜⧓⤛

Market Day and Night

WE RAN into all sorts of funny things in the produce section.

We met a group of egg-candlers in the West Washington Market, passed the time of day with a chiseler (his specialty happened to be meat blocks), and watched river pirates scuttling up and down the Hudson from the decks of the *Thomas Willett* fire-boat at the foot of Little West Twelfth Street.

JOHN CARY, CHISELER

The egg-candlers took their work seriously. With cat-like deftness, they juggled eggs in the darkened room on the second floor of the Armour and Company warehouses at Fourteenth Street and Death Avenue. Tiny shafts of light radiating from electric bulbs placed in hooded standards served to show up the imperfections of the eggs held in front of them.

The solemn-faced gentlemen handle thousands of eggs a day.

"Don't you ever feel tempted to break any?" I asked one of them.

His only reply was an injured look.

"No, they never break any," said E. Stickle, white-aproned manager of Armour and Company.

"How are the eggs graded?" asked Mrs. Steinway.

"By the feel as well as the color and inside quality," answered Mr. Stickle. "Any imperfections are brought out against the light."

West Washington Market begins at Fourteenth Street and Death Avenue. It runs into Gansvoort Market a few blocks below. The first is a wholesale meat, egg, and butter business. The second features live poultry, though early in the morning Long Island farmers assemble in the wide square at Gansvoort Street and West Street for vegetable trading.

There is a great contrast between the cleanliness of the two markets. The meat, butter, and egg end of it, is spick and span. Everything is scrubbed within an inch of its life, including the green hams which are smoked on the premises. The poultry market is a hit-or-miss affair. Live rabbits, ducks, geese, and turkeys are crowded into the sagging red-brick buildings that flank the waterfront. But as far as that goes, all the live poultry markets we ran into were dirty smelly places. The waterfront is infested with them.

A heterogeneous assortment of lunch-rooms and ragtag and bob-tail shacks clustered on the docks in front of the West Washington poultry market. The main eating place carried a huge sign on which was printed "Bathing in the Rear, No Cover Charge."

When we arrived, the waterfront people were fishing for Tomcods.

"Not so very good eating," one of the firemen said. "But it gives them fellows something to do." Work was at a standstill along the water-front docks. "We'll know prosperity is here when the ships start up again," a fireman on the *Thomas Willett* said. Times were hard along the waterfront in the winter of '33.

"Every bed filled," was the sign hung on the door of the Seaman's House Relief Department at West and Jane Streets.

So were the vacant lots. Down-and-outers made temporary sleeping quarters of the space on the northwest corner of Little West Twelfth and Washington Streets. Some twenty or thirty men had burrowed in packing-boxes for winter hibernating.

"But don't you go feel sorry for them boys," the policeman said, joining Mrs. Steinway and myself. "They wouldn't know what to do with work if they got it. This is the life for them. They'd never sleep if you gave them a bed."

We lunched at the Seminole Dining Car opposite the Patchtown settlement. James Ponzio owns it. He's proud of his diner.

"We get them all," he said. "Chorus-girls, big shots and what-have-you. The food is good."

"And clean," said Fireman John J. Nannon, who guided us to the Seminole.

Fireman Nannon has been on duty for thirty-five years. He

remembers the famous Hoboken fire in '99. He's had his share of fires, but not wives.

"Never a girl to look at me," he mourned.

"You firemen are probably too busy to bother with wives," Mrs. Steinway said.

"I hope that's it," he answered.

There are ten fire-boats anchored in local waters. Captain Francis Ryan skippers the *Thomas Willett* at the foot of Little West Twelfth Street. The acting chief is Joseph Riddle. There are one pilot, two engineers, one stoker and a commanding officer on the boat in addition to the firemen. The waterfront averages for them a fire every week or so.

The trick with burning boats is to put out the fire and not sink the ship.

River pirates! Yes, the waters around Manhattan Island are infested with them. But they are not a romantic crew. Far from it. Their boats bear more resemblance to push-carts than a pirate's frigate. And they, themselves, look more like old-clothes men, than counterparts of Captain Kidd.

They hang out on the East River below Fulton Street. They will steal anything and everything. Monkey wrenches, life-preservers, and rope are all grist to their mill. When pick-up days are slack, they work at night, hauling condemned boats across the Hudson to the Jersey shore. It costs money to dispose of an old boat. The government rules that condemned river-craft must be taken to sea and dynamited, an expensive business.

The less reputable ship-owners pay the Fulton river-rats about half the sum to dispose of their condemned boats in local waters, a practice that endangers river-craft. Driftwood from old boats jams propellers and breaks rudders. To guard against the wrecking of ships in local waters, the Government employs a patrol boat, which not only cruises for driftwood but keeps a weather eye out for river pirates.

If you go looking for them, as we did on the South Street docks, you won't find them. They spend their days and nights scuttling up and down the Hudson and East Rivers, like so many water-rats. When they do put into port, it is well after dark.

Great piles of Christmas trees blocked our way as we walked through the Washington Market district. It was the second week in December. New York was making ready for the holidays. The Yuletide cast its shadow not only on the sidewalks but in the markets.

The approaching holidays were evident in the scarlet tissue-paper that trimmed the more exotic food packages such as those displayed by Mr. Joseph, dealer in rare game and meats at the old Washington Market. Neatly set out on his counter, were red-tissue-wrapped plovers from England, prize grouse from Scotland, mallard ducks from Maryland and Ohio partridges.

Alexander, the meat man, proudly exhibited a possum from Virginia and venison from Nova Scotia.

We lunched in the restaurant which Rogers, the clamman, has taken over on the second floor of the market building. It is a quaint place, typical of the 'eighties—the period in which the market house was built. Since Mr. Rogers has tacked his name onto the restaurant, everything has been painted and spruced up. The food is good, particularly the steamed clams and oyster stew; both orders he specializes in at his clam counter, which has been in operation since 1884.

The new World-Telegram Building with the largest city-room in the world, lies one block north of Washington Market at Barclay Street. The telephone company occupies the intervening square.

When excavations were begun on the World-Telegram Building, the hulk of an old square rigger was uncovered. This property is filled-in land. At one time, it must have been years ago, the water extended as far in as Greenwich Street. At some points, especially near St. Paul's and Trinity the river came up even farther. In old books, I run across accounts of the sandy white beaches that stretched a few feet below the church property.

Hevlyn Benson, an old New Yorker, says that his ancestors owned the land now covered by the World-Telegram Building on Barclay and Worth Streets. The Benson farm extended to Dey Street. Benjamin Benson lived on it until 1775, when he signed the "Association test," marking him as a patriot. The British confiscated his property. Benson and his family fled to Haverstraw. They never regained the land. After a succession of owners, the property fell into the hands of the Rhinelanders.

Thirty-Six

The Grapevine Route

HUDSON RIVER STEAMER

WHEN Hendrick Hudson, in 1609, first sailed up the river that now bears his name, the island of Manhattan that he viewed from the deck of the *Half Moon* did not include the site upon which stands the new administration and central office building of the New York Telephone Company. It was then a part of the river bed.

The Dutch West India Company, formed in 1621, claimed all the land on Manhattan Island by virtue of Hudson's discovery. This company set apart a farm or plantation extending from Broadway to the bank of the Hudson River and from Fulton Street to Chambers Street and upon this plot erected a garrison and fort as well as housing quarters for its workmen. In 1664 this land was seized by the British in the name of the Crown and it was called Duke's Farm (1664-1674). Later its name was changed to Ding's Farm (1674-1702) and still later to Queen's Farm (1702-1705).

In 1697 King's Farm was leased by the Crown to the Trinity Church Corporation for seven years, the yearly rental being fifty bushels of wheat. When the lease expired in 1704 Queen Anne granted the land in fee simple to Trinity Church.

As early as 1696 the land with which we are concerned, that on the river bottom in front of the farm, was accounted for by the Great Charter, granted by the English Governor Thomas Dongan, to the colony which even then was referred to as the City of New York. This Charter stated that land under water was held to be the property of the city.

It was not until 1773 that these water lots took on any significance and were deeded as actual property. On November seventeenth of that year, the City of New York transferred title of this land under water to Trinity Church with certain provision for reclaiming the land and the laying out of streets.

Sometime between 1787 and 1800 the sloping highlands were leveled and the shore-line filled so that the land upon which the telephone building rests dates from that time. The filling-in process was done gradually by those who labored to drive the waters of the Hudson back far enough to make it easier for vessels to navigate nearer to the shops and markets in the vicinity.

Both the land granted by the English Crown and the land developed from the water lots deeded by the city remained the property of Trinity Church until 1793. In that year the Church sold two blocks between Greenwich Street and the new boundary of the river (the land having then been filled in) and between Barclay and Vesey Streets to a farmer named Samuel Ellis, who also owned the island in New York Harbor that bears his name. A year later, Ellis died and the property passed to his second wife and her two daughters.

Sometime before 1805 the legal heirs of Samuel Ellis had a map made of Ellis's property by William Bridges, a well-known surveyor of that day. According to this map the heirs disposed of most of the property, selling it in large and small parcels. In 1811 Ellis's heirs sold the northeast corner of Vesey and West Streets and the land along Vesey Street to Joshua Jones, a wealthy member of an old Welsh family. The telephone company bought this land in several parcels and at various times from Jones's heirs, the Pendletons, De Trobriands and others.

The southeast corner of Barclay and West Streets was sold in 1813 by Ellis's descendants to John Anderson, a prosperous merchant of Hackensack, New Jersey. Mr. Anderson's heirs retained it until 1864 when it was sold to Phillip Stark of Brooklyn, from whose devisees the company purchased.

John Anderson also bought the southwest corner of Washington and Barclay Streets at the same time (1813) and it was held by his heirs until 1864 when it was sold to Conrad F. Myer, whose daughter, Mrs. Moller of Brooklyn, sold it to the telephone company. The northwest corner of Washington and Vesey Streets was held by the direct descendants of Samuel Ellis until 1920 when it was purchased from them for the company.

As the city grew the block was soon covered with quaint two-and three-story frame and brick buildings. Many of these structures were haunts of the deep-sea rover and those who came to barter with him. The buildings were constructed one against the other in a helter-skelter fashion, no attention being paid to uniformity or architectural symmetry. There are still a few buildings of similar type farther along West Street.

Shops and stores gave place to other shops and stores doing a small retail business, and until the time when all buildings were demolished to make way for the new structure the block was one of small trade and a favorite spot for retail fruit dealers to peddle wares to passing pedestrians.

Following the work of demolition of the old buildings, which began in May, 1923, hundreds of "sand hogs" started their task of constructing the foundations that extend seventy feet to the solid rock under the old river bottom.

During the work of excavation many relics were found. These included an old boat, a section of a wooden water main, cedar logs, coins, and the skull of a ram. According to a Columbia University geologist the logs indicated that the building site had once been a cedar forest.

Into the holes dug by the sand hogs concrete foundations were placed, twenty-two huge caissons forming the main supports of the building, and to distribute the pressure forty concrete buttresses were provided supporting the foundation walls. Quicksands added to the difficulties and as the lower level was reached, pumping equipment removed as much as two hundred and seventy gallons of intruding water per minute.

About a year after the work of excavation began, an army of workers commenced placing the structural steel for the basement floors and lower walls. Structural steel foundations above the ground level began in the fall of 1924 and before the end of the year the framework had risen fifteen stories, more than one hundred and eighty steel workers toiling night and day for the speedy completion of their part of the building.

Industries and institutions like individuals have their distinctive personalities, and just as a residence reflects the character of its owner, so does the structure which houses the headquarters of any big industry take on something of the personality of that industry. The West Street building represents the combination of American labor and capital in the construction of a new home for an industry that is peculiarly American.

The first ten stories of the building are designed principally for central office uses, while the additional stories and the tower are for administrative office purposes. Space is provided for six full-sized central offices of the machine switching type capable of serving a total of one hundred and twenty thousand telephones.

The exterior of the building is of light buff brick, and the sills, lintels, decorative arches, and panels are limestone. On the ground floor is a corridor of marble and Travatine and an arcade seventeen feet wide which runs the entire length of the Vesey Street side, and marks a new departure in big building construction, but one old to the waterfront. Market arcades have always existed in New York.

Thirty-Seven

❧

An American Hotel and A
Turkish Candy Shop

FREIGHT FERRY BOAT

THE scene of the crime! New York has its share of such spots. Unsolved mysteries! Manhattan Island is rich in them; refutations of the old adage that murder will out.

On our East River walk, we explored the ancient redbrick stable where Ridley, the grizzled-haired, white-bearded dry-goods merchant met his death, in May, 1933.

On the North River, we visited the Glen Island Hotel at the corner of Cortlandt and West Streets, in which Walter Brooks, twenty-one-year-old playboy was shot, on the fourteenth of February, 1902. Both crimes remain unsolved.

The Glen Island Hotel belongs to the golden age that knew the curves of Lillian Russell, the languishing feminine glances of the eyes with the light that lies, and the mustache-twirling boys who said it with champagne. Their stamping-ground was the Glen Island Hotel, an ornately decorated hostelry, famous for its looking-glass ceilings and marble-railed, horseshoe bar.

Half of the bar and all of the ceilings remain intact. W. H. Quick, the former proprietor, is dead. The champagne-drinking patrons have vanished and the thin gray dust of time spreads a fine film over the furniture that once stood in the old hotel.

Most of it is stored, in what was the parlor, on the second floor overlooking West Street. We poked around the room, a snowy afternoon in early December. It was a cold drafty place, bare of floor and musty of air. Great walnut bed-pieces leaned up against the wall. In the lot, I suppose, was the bed from room Number 12—the one in which Brooks was found unconscious.

Mr. Jost, the present proprietor of the Glen Island, is vague as to the details of the murder. Few remember the name of the boy who was killed. The majority have forgotten the girl who was accused of shooting him. Her name was Florence Burns. She had been seen often in company with Brooks. They say she came to the hotel with him that fatal Friday night, that they both registered on the curious old revolving-counter guest-book and that the clerk assigned them room Number 12. Such was the evidence offered by the opposition at the trial. Proof was not great enough to carry the case. Pretty, blonde-haired, nineteen-year-old Florence Burns was acquitted.

Seventeen years later, her name again appeared in the papers. Accused of intoxication and disorderly conduct, she was arrested and paroled, in the custody of her parents. Since her acquittal in the Brooks case, she had served a term for working the badger game.

Such is the grim story of the old Glen Island Hotel. Today it handles casual transients.

Cortlandt Street is a highway that leads to the ferries. The hustle and bustle of hurrying commuters gives it a temporary aspect. Like the tide of some great river, the crowds flow east in the mornings and west at night. The Delaware and Lackawanna, Central Railroad of New Jersey, and West Shore lines shuttle their ferries back and forth from the Jersey shores to this portion of West Street.

The same ferries were churning the waters of the North River in Walter Brooks's day. In fact the woman who shot him was said to have met him in Newark and crossed with him on a Cortlandt Street Ferry to New York.

The former kitchens of the Glen Island Hotel are now occupied by the Carl Thompson fish shop. Mr. Thompson deals in rare varieties of tropical fish. His glass tanks fill the upper and lower floors of the wing in which tidbits for the gay revelers of the Glen Island were prepared.

A half-block down on West Street, just this side of the Liberty Street Ferry, is Mr. Jensen's clock museum. Jensen is the pioneer of the neighborhood. Since 1884, he has been mending watches and clocks for Jersey commuters as well as New York's first families. His heart beats with the thousand-and-one clocks that fill his two-by-four shop. The collection is the result of years' searching on the part of Mr. Jensen for odd and rare time-pieces. A clock that is four hundred years old, another designed for Mary Stuart, watches that chime, mantel clocks made in France during the Napoleonic era, and Copenhagen time-pieces of the seventeenth century are but a few of those that crowd his little store. Offhand he will tell you, as he did Mrs. Steinway and myself, that they are for sale, but if you try to buy any, that is another matter. With the soul of a true collector, he refused, when pressed, to part with his beloved clocks.

MR. JENSEN, THE CLOCK MAN.

In appearance, Mr. Jensen looks like a little gnome, an illusion that is strengthened when he scampers around his room, setting all the clocks to going at once, chimes, bells, music-boxes and all.

There are three generations of Jensens in the store—the elder Mr. Jensen, his son and two grandsons. The grandfather remembers the Glen Island murder tale. One of the high spots of our West Street walk was the call we made upon Mr. Abaid. He is a native of Damascus and an old acquaintance of Mrs. Steinway. His shop is at 53 Washington Street. A vacant lot separates it from the river-front street. Mr. Abaid deals in Syrian confections. His father and mother before him did. It was in their little sweetmeat shop at Damascus that he learned to make the Turkish paste, Oriental pastry and specially prepared nuts which he sells on Washington Street.

The narrow street with its sagging old red-brick houses, towering loft buildings and crowded pavements is home to Nicolas Abaid. He has lived on it twenty-nine years. His five children were born and raised on it. A bell sounded our arrival, when we opened the door to his shop that snowy winter's afternoon we visited Mr. Abaid. It tinkled far back in the rear of the shop. Mr. Abaid came running out, white apron flying, waving a wooden spoon and crying, "Hello, hello, hurry in or my apricot paste will burn!"

We found ourselves racing after him to the kitchen, where a great kettle of rich, red-brown apricot paste bubbled on the stove. It was a critical moment. We held our breath while Mr. Abaid delicately stirred the sugary concoction, gently lifted it from the stove and finally poured it out on a great white marble slab.

He sighed with relief, and laid his spoon down on the counter.

"Now, I can talk," he said. "I have great difficulty trying to make candy. Customers come, I can not work."

The little Abaids were at school. "When they come home, it is simpler," he said. The eldest of them is in New York University.

He is studying to be an electrical engineer. With the children at home, the entire family work in the kitchen and store. Christmas is a busy time with them.

There is Baklawa, the sweet cake, to bake, loloom to prepare and the paste to slice and powder with sugar. It is all very delicious and always fresh. Mr. Abaid pointed to great trays of it, lining his kitchen. Barrels of sugar surrounded us. Huge cans of goat-milk butter stood on the floor and racks of strange-looking pastry filled occasional shelves.

Mrs. Steinway buys her Christmas candies of Mr. Abaid, and her figs and nuts, which come from Damascus straight to Mr. Abaid's store.

He often gets homesick for his own land and people. One day he got out some postcards and showed a friend.

"This is the country where I was born," he said. "I often look at these pictures."

The neighbor was an artist. "I'll paint those on your walls for you," he said. "It will give me something to do these winter evenings."

The friend went to work. His efforts decorate Mr. Abaid's store today. Though naive in conception, the attempt to please Mr. Abaid is evident in the swaying mosques, brooding sheiks, and minaret rooftops of Constantinople and Damascus.

Rose-water and almond paste fill Mr. Abaid's shop with fragrance. His curious star-shaped foreign sweetmeats and pastries emphasize the foreign atmosphere. It is a far cry from West Street and the Abaid store—even though they are but a block apart.

Diagonally across from Mr. Abaid rises the tall shaft of the New York Downtown Athletic Club. Fools rush in where angels fear to tread. Mrs. Steinway and I marched up to the desk in a lobby of modernistic motif.

"Could you tell us something of the history of this building?" we asked.

"Ladies are not allowed in here," the clerk frowned. "It's even more restricted than the Y.M.C.A."

We lingered. "When was it built?"

"Nineteen thirty-one." The clerk glanced at the door.

"Resident house?"

A nod was our answer.

Though originally designed for club-use only, by members, I understand that the Downtown Athletic Club is now open to all men who wish to live on the waterfront in Lower New York.

Thus into a picture that has heretofore known only such lodgings as the substantial but old-fashioned seamen's hotels, has come the first phase of a new era—in the form of a forty-story, fire-proof structure, that commands a view of the length and breadth of Manhattan Island. A deluxe home for men of the waterfront, who have the price. Its only rival on the North River front is the million-dollar Y.M.C.A. Seamen's Institute, at Twenty-First Street and Twelfth Avenue.

Thirty-Eight

The Last Lap

ELLIS ISLAND BOAT

THERE was no blowing of steamboat whistles the afternoon that we finished our waterfront walk. No Grover Whalen committee of welcome greeted us as we put our feet in Battery Park that fifteenth day of December, 1933.

The few people who hurried past us, as we swung from South Street to the Battery Wall paid not the slightest attention to the two, eager-looking women who wore a "Columbus-discovering-America" expression on their faces. And yet, I am sure that no returning hero ever felt more excitement.

"We've actually done it!" exclaimed Mrs. Steinway.

"Walked around Manhattan Island! I wish we were starting all over again."

We stood for a few minutes—looking out over the water. It

was a cold gray day. The steam from the boats floated in clouds made definite by the chilling air. As we watched the river traffic, it began to snow, steadily, slowly, in fine white flakes, that veiled the old fire-house with its absurd little tower, coated the round, cheese-box-like Aquarium building with a thin white film, and shrouded the towering skyscrapers behind us in swirling mists.

The walks around Battery Park were deserted, tiny amusement stands boarded up for the winter and excursion boat offices closed.

We turned to look at the city. Through the falling curtain of snow we could vaguely see State Street, with its row of still-primitive houses snuggling up against huge office buildings.

"I believe the house where my Grandmother Morton lived is standing," Ruth Steinway said. "I think the number is Nine State Street." She leaned forward a little. "Yes, there it is!"

The house was red-brick, five-storied and of the popular nineteenth-century architecture. Tiny, lattice-paned windows gave it a quaint touch.

"I remember driving down here when I was a little girl, in my grandmother's carriage to see that house," Mrs. Steinway continued. "She lived there as a child."

Adjoining the old Morton house is the Mission of Our Lady of the Rosary, formerly the home of Moses Rogers, New York's wealthiest merchant in the first part of the nineteenth century. Father Temple, the nice Irish priest in charge of the mission, has been busy restoring it this past year. The white columns in front, the black iron railing and the pink Colonial bricks have been retouched.

Also in this row of old houses is the place where Honest Bill Quigley, boatman of the Battery, was born.

"I want you to meet Mr. Quigley," I said to Ruth Steinway. "Let's walk over to the Statue of Liberty ferry-house and see if he is calling on Buck McNeil."

"Who is Buck McNeil?" answered Mrs. Steinway.

"He's the volunteer life-saver of the Battery. They say he's saved more than two hundred and fifty lives."

"And Mr. Quigley?"

"Everybody down here knows him. His boat is over in that basin." I pointed to a little walled-in basin at the far end of the Battery.

We stepped into a warm room at the ferry-house. A group of old-timers were toasting their feet in front of the heater, smoking pipes and swapping yarns.

A big, husky-looking Irishman with a pipe stuck in one corner of his mouth and a smile that swept from ear to ear, moved forward. It was Buck McNeil.

"And sure ye've just missed Bill," he said. "Quigley is after leaving about ten minutes."

Buck invited us to stay—talked a little of the Old Hound Guards, that historic neighborhood organization which he revived, and wished us the season's greetings when we said we had to be moving on.

Winter or summer, the Battery is a fascinating spot.

At the far end is Quigley's basin, beyond that is the ferry to Ellis Island, the United States Cutter service docks, the Governor's Island Ferry, and the ferry to Staten Island.

The Government buildings are modern enough in appearance.

The Staten Island ferry-house is of an earlier architecture, a type that Walt Whitman has immortalized in his poems. The old weather-beaten sheds, the reek of the wharves, the grind of the cog-wheels as the boat slips into dock, impress sight, smell and hearing.

Past and present are closely linked at Battery Park. The kaleidoscopic shifting of coastlines and buildings is not new. Thomas A. Janvier, in referring to changes that have taken place at the Battery, writes: "Meanwhile there had been set up in this region another military engine of destruction which never came to blows with anybody, but led always a life of peaceful useful-ness that is not yet at an end. This was the Southwest Battery that later was to be known honorably as Castle Clinton; that still later was to become notable, and then notorious, as Castle Garden; and then at the present time is to take a fresh start in respectability as the Aquarium.

"It is not easy to realize nowadays, as we see this chunky little fort standing on dry ground that when it was built between the years of 1807 and 1811, it was a good hundred yards from shore. Battery Park was a crescent-shaped piece of land which ended at the waterside in a little bluff, capped by a wooden fence with a shining beach beyond."

The huge doors of the Aquarium are of an age with the build-ing. They are the doors of the fort and were constructed to with-stand cannon fire. Another character of the Battery is William Flanagan, the clam man. In his district, he is as well-known as Patrick O'Connor, the clam man of Coenties Slip.

From the Statue of Liberty ferry house, we pushed our way against wind and snow to the far end of the Battery and Mr.

Flanagan's stand. His little stall was closed. The storm had sent him home.

Thirty-Nine

The End and the Beginning

BATTERY PARK was blanketed in white when we officially ended our tour. The brown earth, seared grass and bare trees were covered with snow.

Our farewell salute was a brisk toot-toot from the *Dalzettea*, flag-ship of the Dalzell tug-fleet. Bobbing at anchor off the Battery Wall, Captain Howell's boat brought a cheerful touch to what might otherwise have been a melancholy finish to our walk.

"I wish we were just starting out," said Mrs. Steinway. "I should like to be beginning all over again."

"Toot-toot!" sounded the tug.

"Let's go over and take a look at it," I suggested.

The Dalzell fleet does most of the docking and undocking of the battle-ships in the Brooklyn Navy Yard. It also deals in trans-atlantic vessels. Often as many as six or seven of the sturdy little boats will bring in a big ocean liner.

The tugs get orders wigwagged to them from the offices of the company on the tenth floor of 21 State Street, across Battery Park.

The *Dalzellea* was waiting for papers when we saw her. She is the pride of the fleet, has a crew of eight men, a cook and sleeping quarters for the sailors when they work overtime. Often they get orders to bring in a boat at midnight, if a fog happens to be lifting.

Tugboat captains are important people. When the docking of a ship is especially difficult, Captain Howell often turns the wheel of his own boat over to the mate, while he climbs the bridge of the big liner to pilot it to the wharf.

To most of us, the running of a tug seems an idyllic occupa-tion, but the dangers of the river and harbor are many. Burning ships, heavy weather, shifting channels and low tides are always a menace.

A tugboat captain must know the river in all its moods. Often a tug will be caught between a ship and a pier; a bad tide, a sudden shift of the wind—the plucky harbor fighter is crushed like so much papier-mache and sent to Davy Jones's locker.

The captains are gallant, courageous and quick-thinking. It's all in a day's work: ice, storms, fogs, wrecks, fires and being nice to the ladies.

As we neared the *Dalzellea*, Captain Howell caught sight of us, from the pilot-room. Shouting to one of his men to help us on board, he climbed down to the main deck.

There is no extra space on tugs. They are built for action. The one cabin where the men can gather is the galley. It is a homey spot, with the big table, always set, the red-and-white-checked cloth; the cook stove near by with soup pots simmering, and the chef—who usually knows his business—on guard. Tugboat men demand and get good food.

"What about cruising around and seeing the harbor a little?" suggested Captain Howell.

"No thanks, not to-day," I said. "I just wanted Mrs. Steinway to meet you and the tug."

We climbed up to the pilot-room, examined the big wheel, peered out over the bay—the storm blotted out the Statue of Liberty—inspected the powerful engines and sampled the cook's coffee.

The harbor widens out into the bay below the Battery. The little boats that connect with near-by islands leave from South Ferry. From the *Dalzellea* we could see crowds hurrying to the Staten Island boats. The Governor's Island Ferry is not so popular. Only officers, their families and friends are permitted on board. Governor's Island is but a short sail from New York. The old fortress, a duplicate of the Aquarium building, marks it. We could barely distinguish it through the storm.

The New York of the past was more familiar with the island now owned by the United States. Its Indian name was Pagganck, or Nut Island. The Dutch lengthened it into Noton or Nutten Island because of the chestnut crop in the autumn.

Wouter Van Twiller was its original purchaser from the Indians. He used it as his private property, as he did the Great Barn and Little Barn Islands, now known as Ward's and Randall's. The Dutch Government ordered Peter Stuyvesant to take Nutten Island over as public property. During the occupation of New York by the English, Lord Cornbury built himself a magnificent mansion on Nutten Island. It was not until after the American Revolution began that fortifications were ordered erected on it, alternately by the British and American forces. After peace was declared, Governor Clinton came into possession of it. He leased it for the purposes of a race course and a hotel. Fashionable New York flocked to it for relaxation. But its gaiety was short-lived. When war with Great Britain again threatened the young Republic, the island was fortified by volunteers from the city. It was while the War of 1812 raged that the grim cheese-box-like fortress which landmarks it, was erected. The old building is in use today as a military prison.

During the reign of Governor Clinton, Nutten Island became known as Governor's Island. Since then it has been occupied bj the United States Army. The commanding officer is head of the Army of the East.

No waterfront picture is complete without tugboats. They date back to the days when more sails than smokestacks dotted the harbor.

New York was a big town then—I'm speaking of the eighties and 'nineties—even then it was America's greatest port of entry, but to the ships that nosed through the Narrows, Manhattan

Island, minus its awe-inspiring steel and concrete sky-line must have looked merely like a sleepy, peaceful, seaport community. Trinity spire was then the highest point on the island. A forest of skyscrapers blotted it out when we tried to catch a glimpse of it from the decks of the *Dalzellea*.

In the brief span of forty years, since tugboats have been churning through the harbor, the spire of Trinity has been buried by the massive buildings that have transformed New York from an overgrown country town into the greatest city in the world.

Side by side with the miraculous physical development of New York has been the equally miraculous growth of her shipping. Today, New York is not only the world's greatest city, but the world's greatest seaport.

Without pause, the ebb and flow of business and human life etches an intricate pattern on the waterfront. Endless traffic— ships, cargo-laden; a painter turns to the river-front for atmosphere, the city's big newspapers comb the docks for stories—the stream of life stems on, moving, swiftly fascinating in its course. A course that you can follow if you take to the water-front.

The *Dalzellea* sounded its whistle in a farewell blast as we climbed back over the wooden pierheads, to the Battery Wall.

It was the salute of one friend to another. Mrs. Steinway and I had been recognized by a waterfront veteran, an important citizen of the harbor—the tugboat. We were waterfront people.

"If it gets into your blood, you'll never get it out," Captain Gully's words rang in my ears. "Ye'll always be following the waterfront."

THE END

I am indebted to the World-Telegram for permission to use the portion of this book which appeared in a series of articles in that paper.

Index

www.ingramcontent.com/pod-product-compliance
Lightning Source LLC
Chambersburg PA
CBHW032125020426
42334CB00016B/1070